SPHERE COLOUR PLANT GUIDES
FLOWERS
FOR THE HOME

SPHERE BOOKS LIMITED
London and Sydney

CONTENTS

Production: Inmerc BV, Wormer (Netherlands) and Mercurius Horticultural Printers, 11 East Stockwell Street, Colchester, Essex
Text: Kathe Dobie
Photography: Fleurmerc, Wormerveer (Netherlands); Flower Council of Holland, Leyden (Netherlands); Verenigde Bloemen-veilingen Aalsmeer (Netherlands); D. van Raalte
Photo cover: Harry Smith
Layout: Inmerc BV, Wormer (Netherlands)
Typesetting: RCO/Telezet BV, Velp (Netherlands)
Printing: BV Kunstdrukkerij Mercurius-Wormerveer (Netherlands)
This edition published by Sphere Books Ltd., 30-32 Gray's Inn Road, London WCIX 8JL
© 1985 Mercbook International Ltd., Guernsey

INTRODUCTION

There are few sights in the world to rival the glory of a garden in full bloom.

This book aims to tell you how you can bring the colour and fragrance of the garden into your home – and preserve them for all year round enjoyment.

Modern growing techniques and rapid transport links mean that nowadays you can also enjoy the most exotic blooms from all over the world.

The cost of labour, transport and heating involved in producing many of them, however, means that these exotic flowers which tempt you into the florist's shop will often be very highly-priced.

There will be occasions upon which you will be happy to pay – and to ensure that you get the best we tell you all about those tropical blooms and what to look for when buying.

But it is quite possible to use your own garden to produce splendid blooms to brighten up the home all year round. Some can be cut in the garden and displayed fresh in vases. Others can be dried to retain their colour and fragrance or made into potpourris or pomanders to give a constant reminder of the smells of spring and summer in the depths of winter.

This book will tell you all you need to know about cut and dried flowers. We explain about the professional flower grower, what he produces and tell you when you can expect to find the various commercially-grown blooms in the shops.

We explain how best to prepare your plot and how to grow a whole range of glorious flowers.

There are sections on how to get the best out of your cut flowers, how to prepare them and on the art of arranging.

We also tell you how to select the best blooms when picking or buying from the shops.

There is a section on drying flowers which explains fully all the best methods for extending the life and scent of your flowers.

And we tell you all about those sadly underrated wild flowers which can give your garden a romantic, uninhibited, wild look as well as give your home some delightful natural colour and foliage.

The most important chapter of the book lists some 103 flowers with their full details. We tell you how to grow them, what height they reach, the colour of their flowers, how to treat them and when you will find them in the shops.

You may not be able to take your garden indoors with you but with the aid of this book you will be able to bring the fragrance and the colour of the garden into your home, and keep them there, for as long as you wish.

PROFESSIONAL CULTURE

Growing flowers on a commercial basis is big business – though much bigger in other parts of Europe and the world than it is in the U.K. Unquestionably the market leader is Holland where, though the climate may not match that of competitors like Israel and Central America, the vast network of greenhouses that can be seen snaking across the low flatlands testifies to an enormous commitment to cut flowers and pot plants. So vital is this business to the economy that some fear the growing trend for home cultivation to be a long-term threat to the financial health of the nation.

Historically Holland's domination of the market lies in a unique partnership between all those involved in the production and marketing of flowers.

Producers, distributors, researchers, experimental stations and all the other experts are involved in a joint venture. Dutch flower people, they will tell you proudly, believe in co-operation.

At one time Europe's markets lay wide open to this rare blend of commercial partnership. Nowadays, however, soaring fuel costs involved in keeping those greenhouses heated plus the rapid development of fast, international transport links, mean that these markets are becoming more and more accessible to hot countries which don't need to heat costly greenhouses, since the heat comes free of charge from the sun.

Holland, now with a stagnant internal market and stiff competition outside, faces a bigger than ever threat to its domination but it is one which the Dutch seem to relish, refusing to indulge in petty trade tariffs or import red tape. Their attitude appears to be that competition truly is good for you. Normally, increased competition would lead to a better deal for the customer. In Holland, in fact, this is true. Prices are among the lowest in the world.

In the U.K. however, imports are enormous and the high fixed costs of transport, heating and labour are passed on to the customer. Cut flowers represent a significant cost and, thus, a greater incentive to grow your own.

As a result of all this, per capita spending in the U.K. is around 20 per cent of spending a head in Holland.

In the U.K. flower crop production involves some 1,300 acres under glass and 2,200 in open fields. In Holland comparative figures are 11,000 acres under glass and 3,000 acres in open fields.

Dutch flower cultivation ranges across a wide assortment of varieties cultivated all year round in heated greenhouses. The most common are roses, chrysanthemums, carnations, freesia, gerberas, tulips, lilies, cymbidiums and irises.

The main pot plants grown include begonias, yucca, ficus, african violet, dieffenbachia, azalea, euphorbia pulcherrima, codiaeum, dracaena and nephrolepsis.

In the U.K. fewer varieties are produced. The chrysanthemum is by far the most valuable while narcissus and daffodil are probably the most commonly bought.

Other varieties include freesia, carnations, roses, irises and gladioli. The U.K. is particularly noted for its production of bulbs giving eight times as much space to bulbs as it does to the cultivation of cut flower crops. In terms of total exports Holland stands out on its own taking some 59 per cent of the world market according to the latest figures available.

As an indication of its dominance, here are the comparative shares of other significant exporters. Denmark and Colombia come second with just 7 per cent each, Israel comes third with 6 per cent.

Italy, Belgium and Luxembourg come 4th with 5 per cent while Central America and West Germany both have a 2 per cent share of the world market. France, Spain, the U.S.A., Thailand and Kenya all have 1 per cent of the market.

It should be pointed out, however, that export figures have little to do with total production. The U.S.A. has a vast internal market and has little obvious need to spend high sums on reaching far-away European markets.

The most commonly produced flowers are roses, carnations, chrysanthemums and gerberas. Holland produces the most roses and gerberas, Italy the most carnations and Japan the most chrysanthemums.

Beside these main cut flower and pot plant producing nations there are many others producing and exporting, though on a much smaller scale. They include Greece, Portugal, Norway, Sweden, Finland, Tunisia, Egypt, Mexico, Argentina etc.

As you can imagine, with all these nations producing and exporting cut flowers and pot plants, the range available in the shops all the year round is fairly diverse.

In 1981 a thousand million pounds worth of nursery products were exported world wide. The export of cut flowers was greater than the export of pot plants.

Rose, chrysanthemum and carnation are the top three international flowers, sold all over the world.

The speedy transport links around the world mean that a pot plant grown, say, on the Ivory Coast, could be in your shop a mere couple of days later. It is small wonder that, during the time that the unfavourable climates of northern Europe inhibit the commercial production of some varieties, tropically-grown cut flowers and pot plants tend to dominate in the shops.

In most northern European countries the level of investment required to start the commercial production of a crop is often the critical factor. The price that a cut flower may make in the shops might mean that some crops would, eventually, be more profitable but they will require far greater investments.

Investing all that money and then having a long wait for the crops to mature, reach the shops and produce a profit may often be far too much to contemplate. This is why simpler, less costly flowers and plants are often grown in preference to ones which might cost far more once available. Such factors tend to dominate the commercial decisions. So, too, does the question of a long vase life. This is definitely the key to the consumers' decision about what to buy. Attractiveness is obvious immediately but if the flower lasts no time at all in the vase then it will probably not be bought again. Blooms which are cut or pulled when they are still too immature usually have a shortened vase life and the same applies to those cut or pulled too late.

Once they have been harvested they will be stood in deep water in a cool place to condition them before being sent to market. With some varieties, gerberas for instance, it is necessary to pull or cut them straight into water or a preserving solution.

Generally growers will hold cut flowers in a bud opening solution at a temperature of 10-15°C and at a humidity of 80-90 per cent.

Growers are always keen to hear about experiments with new cut flower crops but are usually less keen to invest money in them. It is often the case that a producer will take a gamble with a new crop and consequently steal a profitable march on the rest of the industry, but the general rule is that once a new crop has hit the headlines it is probably too late for the rest of the growers to try and catch up. Conservatism is instinctive in the cut flower industry.

However, experimental stations and growers are currently trying one or two new varieties on a commercial scale. These include alstroemeria, antirrhinums, bells of Ireland, bouvardia, campanula, delphiniums, gerberas, gypsophila, liatris, pinks, statice, stocks and sweet williams. Others, such as agapanthus, solidago and centaurea are still being tested for their commercial application. In the U.K. however, it is hard to see any signs of a significant drift away from the dependence on bulbs, bulb flowers and chrysanthemums as the main crops. The major area is given over to bulbs which are brought into flower earlier than normal in heated glasshouses during the winter months. In the west country and the Channel Islands flower-growing in the open is still important, mild winters allowing the production of early crops.

The first narcissi from the Isles of Scilly and Jersey and from the heated greenhouses of the east of England, appear in late November. In the New Year more hot-house narcissi and daffodils appear, followed by main crops from the open, climaxing in a flood of blooms from March to April and finishing in May with the Scottish daffodils. Tulips usually start a bit later, just in time for Christmas, ending in May. Irises will come in June and overlap with gladioli which start in early June and end in late October.

Such is the scale of the gardening boom that plants can be bought all over the place from market stalls to garden centres and from bazaars to supermarkets.

Plants are such appealing things that you can buy on impulse and regret it later.

A lot of poor quality produce is sold from market stalls for this very reason. Impulse buyers attracted by the low cost hand over hard-earned cash and, because of the transient nature of market stall holders, may not get the chance to go back and complain. On the other hand, if the produce is good then it will usually be very good value for money.

The once traditional high street garden shop is slowly disappearing as the department store, supermarket and garden centre take over. This is not always such a good thing. Residing in the more traditional shops is often a vast fund of knowledge built up over the years and there to be taken advantage of by the customer. This, sadly, is often not the case with department stores and supermarkets. These sort of places tend to employ people with little knowledge of the subject. On the other hand, the vast economies of scale often give them the price edge that is slowly killing off the traditional shop. They do have to cope, however, with the problems of centralised packaging and purchasing which means that

their products are designed for longer shelf life than in garden centres and the garden shops. Sometimes plants will be packaged in polythene which all but obscures your ability to check on what sort of quality you are getting.

Like most competing areas of trade, there are advantages and disadvantages on all sides. The general rule, however, must be to buy your plants and flowers where they are well-displayed so that you can thoroughly examine them. Whether they are expensive cut flowers, which last only a short time – and therefore need to be at peak perfection – or bedding plants which you will be caring for in your own garden, there is no point in saving a few pence if the result is a major disappointment later.

Bedding plants. Check to see that the leaves are firm and free from any tell-tale holes or spots. Try and avoid buying plants which are thin – growth should be bushy. Thin plants often mean that they have been grown in too much heat and too little light. Check also that there aren't any roots growing through the bottom of the pot or seed tray. The soil in the pot should be moist and young plants should not be in full flower. Don't buy half-hardy plants before mid-May.

Container grown plants. Perennials grown in containers should have been grown as seedlings or cuttings, potted on and then placed in the whale-hide or plastic pots in which you buy them. A bad supplier may try to sell you one which has been lifted from open ground and crammed into a container. Check for various tell-tale signs: wilted leaves, dense weed growth, dry soil, split container or thick roots growing through the base.

Bulbs. Select firm, mould-free bulbs which have no holes or growing shoots. Don't buy undersized bulbs. Outdoor hyacinths, however, should be bought in medium-sizes and not large. Do not buy bulbs if they are covered in withered scales.

Roses. Generally-speaking you will be buying bare-root plants in autumn or spring which are dormant and packed in peat. If the rose is packed in polythene make sure you can get a good look at the stem before buying. There should be no leafy shoots starting to grow.

Pre-packaged plants. Supermarkets and department stores these days often tend to sell pre-packaged plants in polythene bags. They have a longer shelf life than those you might find in a garden shop or nursery. Usually they will be bare-rooted with a moist peat, sphagnum moss or compost base round the roots. They will generally be cheaper than similar plants sold elsewhere, but beware. You often cannot see well what it is that you are buying and any warmth in the shop may have started premature growth.

Cut flowers. When buying cut flowers it will pay you to try and develop a good relationship with your florist. Cut flowers are unfortunately such a price these days that you might need to examine every costly bloom you buy. Getting them from someone you trust helps.

IN YOUR OWN GARDEN

One of the biggest problems for the home gardener is finding a satisfactory balance between growing vegetables, herbs, fruit and flowers. Increasingly, nowadays, the modern home has a small garden and this places a premium on space. Such demands make it all the more critical that careful consideration and planning go into the design of your garden. It is no good simply planting away merrily and later discovering that you have no room for important plants.

Later in this section we will be giving you detailed advice on the best ways of making use of your space.

For most people, however, a flower border is a must when planning a garden, and it is this traditional garden feature that provides most of the colour and most of the cut flowers which are found in the home. Two mistakes, frequently made, can seriously spoil a mixed plant border or herbaceous border.

The first is lack of good soil preparation, which is dealt with in our section on *Plot and Care*. The second, as we have already suggested, is poor planning.

To make the most of your border, especially if you lack space, you must give careful thought to two important factors. The first is successional planting which involves planning for new varieties to replace others as they die. Try and ensure that your border doesn't go bare in parts by planning for a steady process of replacement. Our detailed section listing individual plants and their various characteristics will be a great help in this. The second major factor is compatibility. This is something on which it is much harder to advise. Common sense and experience will help to tell you which plants go best together. In some cases, of course, it will be quite obvious that you won't let a tall growing plant overshadow a small one or let a bushy plant grow in front of a tiny, frail one. Bear in mind; hedging plants take a lot of nourishment so don't plant too close to them; when planning, contrast and harmonise not only the flowers but the foliage since this will be evident for longer; plant, too, for height and spread; move plants in October where possible since moving during dormant periods like December and January delays root formation.

Perennials, like peonies, lupins, delphiniums, phlox and Michaelmas daisies, play a big part in stocking an herbaceous border since they are more permanent than annuals, reach maturity quicker and grow well with shrubs and vigorous bush roses. Most perennials benefit from lifting every three years or so, and this gives you the added advantage of being able to indulge in a spot of re-planning

and re-organisation. But if the perennials are the more permanent feature of your border, it is the annuals which provide the changing life and variety. They also provide an almost inexhaustible variety of flowers for cutting.

Any attempt to give a full list would be futile but here is a tiny selection of ideas, all of them annuals which are ideal for cutting over a long period. Delphiniums, chrysanthemums, rudbeckia, coreopsis, clarkia, nigella, calendula, brachycome, gilia, nemophilia, helipterum, arctosis, cosmos, linum, eschscholtzia. Herbaceous plants suffer little from pests and diseases, require minimum spraying with insectictides or fungicides,

may need watering in dry weather and will usually grow vigorously if they are given a feed in the spring with a well-balanced fertilizer containing nitrogen, phosphate and potash. Keep them weed-free and in autumn cut the stems of deciduous plants down to just above ground level.

If you do have a premium on space then don't despair – there are four main ways in which you can make the most of what space you do have and even the smallest garden can be exploited to grow a regular succession of blooms.

* Grow plants in pots, tubs or other containers.
* Grow plants which reach upwards rather than outwards.

* Grow plants successionally and in tiers to capitalise upon space.
* Grow plants that are naturally small.

Pots and tubs. The advantage here is that almost any space on the ground or above it can be used. Areas of concrete can take tubs, pots or buckets. They can also be suspended above ground. Grow bags, which also beat soil-borne diseases, are ideal. Almost anything can be grown in this way from tulips and daffodils in the spring to dahlias which will still be flowering in the autumn when the frosts start.

Upwards. You might suppose that this section would be restricted to what are known as climbers, but not so. There are indeed some magnificent climbing plants like clematis, honeysuckle, wistaria and sweet peas. But there is also a wide variety of shrubs which can be trained up walls and trellises. For instance pyracanthus, cotoneaster, ceanothus, hydrangea petiolaris, jasminum nudiflorum and passiflora coerulea (the only species hardy enough to be grown out of doors in most parts of northern Europe).

Successionally and in tiers. If you only have a very small space, or want to really pack as much as you can into what space you have, then do so by a combination of successional planting and planting in tiers. Bulbs, corms and tubers are ideal for this. In spring come the daffodils, tulips, crocuses and chionodoxa, and when they finish in May they make way for flowering herbaceous perennials which start in late April. Roses and fuchsias can be programmed into the scheme for flowering in late spring through to the summer. Dahlias can be planted to take over in late summer from the early flowering perennials. It's all a question of planning. Remember, however, that successional planting can be very costly in plants and in time.

Small. Small varieties of plants which are usually larger include dwarf Michaelmas daisies like 'Audrey', 'Lady in Blue', 'Little Pink Beauty' and 'Snowspite'. Campanula 'Pouffe' is a small, neat variety of the usually tall-growing campanula lactiflora. There are plenty of small-flowering plants which can give you colourful blooms.

PLOT AND CARE

Annuals

Both in the garden and as cut flowers annuals have a number of advantages. There is a great diversity in type and colour, they can be produced in large quantity relatively cheaply and cutting them often encourages the development of further blooms. Annuals are those plants which grow from seed in one year and can generally be fitted into one of two categories: (a) half-hardy annuals which need to be sown in heat either in frames or under glass and (b) hardy annuals which can be sown outside. Of the two, obviously, the latter group is the most popular. The prime requirement of annuals is for an open but reasonably protected site in the sun. The soil should be well-drained, reasonably well-cultivated and fairly rich. Dig in a good barrow load of well-rotted compost for every ten square yards when preparing the site.

Make sure you have completed all the digging at least a month before you intend to sow to give the soil time to settle down.

Annuals can be sown in spring in the open ground (March to April) but not when the soil is sticky. They like very fine soil. With some annuals an autumn sowing can be made in which case select a well-sheltered spot.

Avoid getting your seedlings too large before winter sets in

Annuals are ideal to give your garden a 'new look' every year.

because frosts can kill larger, succulent plants, when sturdy dwarf ones survive.

To allow ease of picking try and make your beds the sort of size over which you can easily reach or step.

Sowing depths will depend on the size of the seed but always sow thinly and thin vigorously. Regular hoeing between rows, or a good mulch, will keep down weeds and help to retain moisture.

Perennials

These are plants which can be grown out of doors, usually without the need for protection. If grown properly and looked after, they will reward you with blooms for many years.

The seeds of hardy perennials

can be sown either in a frame or in an outdoor, reasonably sheltered spot. Sowing times will vary from plant to plant but they will usually be between April and mid-June. Hardy perennials are not usually allowed to flower in the first year.

Keep the soil light but enriched with a light dressing of well-rotted compost about 6 inches down. If the soil is dry it should be watered copiously the afternoon before a morning sowing. Sow thinly to ensure sturdier plants and to save wasteful thinning later. Sowings will usually be half an inch deep but with some perennials it may be as much as one inch. Cover carefully with fine soil dispersing any ridges. If sowing out of doors protect your seedlings from birds with netting.

When they have grown to about three inches – somewhere around one month after sowing – transplant into beds in the open and in a sunny spot. Hoe regularly through the summer or mulch the rows with sedge peat or something similar. You can plant on into the final growing positions in the autumn of the first season but many gardeners leave this until the autumn of the second season.

Chrysanthemums

This plant has so many varieties, flowering from late July until October, that if well-treated and planted selective-ly, it can give your garden and home blooms for a lengthy period. It also has the virtue of being one of the longest-lasting cut flowers in water. Preparing the soil is vital in growing chrysanthemums. Double digging is best, forking in a good layer of farmyard manure into the top spit. They are not deep rooting and like their nourishment near to the surface. Add bone meal or hoof and horn at the rate of 2 oz per square yard and sprinkle on some wood ashes if available. This all helps to make strong, colourful blooms. Some varieties may suffer if left out over winter. Consult your garden shop when buying. In this case they can be lifted.

Place in soil in a cold frame, ventilate except during frosts and keep moist. Plant out the following spring.

Bulbs, corms, rhizomes, tubers

Bulbous plants are among the easiest to grow but for the very best results they need careful handling.

They will do well in almost any well-drained garden soil which has been enriched with organic matter to a depth of about 8 inches to nourish their deeply-penetrating roots. When they pass their peak of blooming dead-head and allow the foliage to die down naturally. Never leave faded or dead petals to drop. Removing the flower heads

Beautiful in the border, beautiful in a vase.

always the most successful. It won't work, for instance, when trying to increase the stock of named varieties of garden origin. The tendency here will be for the plants to revert to their original species.

Increasing from seed will, however, be quite successful when it involves natural species and strains of mixed colours. Some perennials reproduce well from seed too. Make sure your seed bed is protected by a cold frame to protect the seedlings from the worst weather conditions. As temperatures rise the glass can gradually be raised to allow plants to harden off.

Exact reproduction of a plant, however, requires one of a number of types of vegetative reproduction. The easiest is division. This, again, may not be the most satisfactory. Consult the information given in the central section of this book which lists individual plants and their growing needs.

Division is, as it sounds, merely a method of dividing the roots. For this reason it works best with plants that have a strong, mat-forming root system. It must be done with care. Two garden forks can be used to prize the root system apart or it can be done by gently tugging. The easiest plants to divide include perennials like chrysanthemum maximum, phlox, rudbeckia, golden rod and michaelmas daisy.

When you have divided the

and allowing the foliage to die down gives the plants the chance to restore energy for the next growing season. Usually bulbs, tubers etc. can be left in the ground over the winter for flowering the next season. It is a good idea, however, to check every two or three years so that thick clumps can be cleaned and divided. Lift only when foliage has died down. If storing is necessary do so in a cool, airy, frost-free place. Replant the following planting season.

Propagation

It is not only more satisfying but it is considerably cheaper to raise your own plants than to buy them in a garden shop or centre. Increasing stock from seed, nature's way, is the easiest method though it is not

Window-boxes filled with annuals.

plant always try and replant immediately so the shoots do not dry out. If you have been careful they should settle quickly back into the soil. Plants which form a thick, close root system may have to be carefully cut into portions. Make sure that each portion you intend to replant has one or two strong buds on it.

Some perennials have rhizomatous roots – iris germanica for instance – and these can be divided by cutting or breaking the roots cleanly, making sure that buds are on the pieces to be replanted.

Another method of increasing some plants is by detaching young offsets – the tufted development extending from the plant stem at soil level. Either pull off gently or cut off and plant up. This can be done with plants like primroses, hardy geraniums and auriculas. Many bulbous plants can be increased in the same fashion. Narcissus and tulip, among others, produce many new bulbs.

These can be detached and planted up. The same applies to crocuses, gladioli and montbretias among others. With hard and semi-hard wooded plants the technique of layering is usually the most effective. Raise the soil level one inch around the plant to be increased by adding to it a mixture of equal parts loam, silver sand and moss fibre.

Remove leaves from the part of the stem you intend to use and insert a sharp knife point just below a joint. Draw the knife up at an angle through the joint and to about half an inch beyond. Slide the knife through and out. There should now be a sort of tongue. Clean the end of this and bend it down into the soil mixture so that the cut is kept open. Peg it into position to encourage rooting.

Perhaps the most common method of increasing plants, however, is by taking cuttings. These can be taken from stem, root or even, on occasions, from a leaf. The great majority of hardy perennials can be increased in this way. Some plants will root much more easily than others but to help them root the ideal conditions include a moist atmosphere, a good rooting compound and an effective drainage material at the bottom of the pan or pot. Take your cuttings from strong, young growths during the height of the growing season. Do not make them too long though they should be sufficiently long to stand successfully in the rooting compound.

Planning

When planning your flower garden or border, bear in mind that it can, and usually will, be left undisturbed for as much as four years. Make sure therefore that you plan carefully to avoid having to do unnecessary remedial work. Select a well-drained site since this, probably more than any other factor, is something that almost all plants demand.

If your garden tends to be clogged and damp, then dig in plenty of organic material. Don't simply go to a garden centre and buy a selection of seeds and haphazardly start planting. Think about how they will look when flowering. Consult our central section of individual listings for information on height, colour and planting needs. Your aim should be to devise a growing plan which will, as far as possible, ensure a continuous series of blooms all of which go well together.

It may be right to plant taller flowers at the back of a bed but don't be too uniform about your planting. Aim for a border or bed which is constantly providing you with new sights and different angles. Try and cultivate little dells and sections of special interest. Routine, uniform planting may be easy but you have to live with your flower bed for a long time so try and make it interesting. In most average-sized gardens you won't have the luxury of being able to plant special beds of perennials, annuals, bulbs and shrubs and will more than likely be growing a mix. In this case it is all the more important to see that you are selecting ones that grow well together and that will compliment each other when they are blooming.

The main aims in cultivating your own flower garden should be to provide yourself with the pleasure of colour in the garden throughout the year, while at the same time providing a succession of cut flowers to brighten up the house. In a garden of average size this should be quite possible if it is properly prepared and stocked – and it should not require an undue amount of attention.

Flowers and foliage from at least March to October are a perfectly realistic aim for the amateur gardener, and if you should choose to go in for everlastings and for indoor bulbs this can be extended well into winter giving a supply for the home for the major part of the year.

To be successful, however, requires a certain amount of effort in preparing the correct soil. If you are hoping to produce a continuous series of blooms it stands to reason that your raw material, the soil, will have to be up to the task. It is not possible to continue extracting goodness from the soil - to produce your blooms – without putting it back.

The key here is keeping up a good supply of natural humus. The use of chemicals is generally to be frowned upon in a flower garden because it unbalances the soil. Ensuring a good supply of humus will generally take care of the needs of soil and plants alike ensuring good, healthy growth which is resistant to disease.

Organic material, like the unwanted parts of plants, lawn cuttings, weeds, sweet pea haulms, etcetera, can be rotted down on your compost heap and added to the soil when digging the plot. The carbonic acid produced by this organic matter helps to release phosphates and potash to enrich the soil.

It also improves water retention which improves light soil, and it makes heavier soil easier to work. Incorporate this organic material into your soil in spring and autumn at the rate of one good barrow load for every 10 square yards. Fork it in no deeper than 6 inches. You can also use it as a top dressing or mulch along the rows of annuals and perennials.

Other good organic substances include sea-weed, fish manure, dried blood, hoof and horn and even soot.

Your soil may be deficient in some degree or other and to correct this there is a variety of fertilisers on the market. First, however, you will have to know about the needs of your soil and your plants.

Three main elements are required for good soil and successful growth. Nitrogen is vital in developing new growth and a shortage of it shows in slow, stunted growth and pale leaves.

Potassium or potash improves the quality of plants making

them stronger and more disease resistant and adding colour and extra life to the flowers. A shortage of potash shows itself in pale-yellow or brown leaves. Phosphates are important for root production and help plants to grow to maturity more rapidly. Any shortage will often show itself in stunted growth and red or purplish leaves.

A good soil will contain all these elements and more which are needed for successful plant growth. Watch out, however, for these tell-tale signs or, if you are concerned, buy one of the many soil testing kits which are available on the market. This will give you a reliable guide to the minerals which are and are not in your garden soil.

Should you need to correct an imbalance then there is a variety of organic fertilisers available.

Fertilisers

If your soil or plants show signs of deficiency then select the fertiliser which will correct this.

Bear in mind, however, that organic fertilisers take some time to work. That is why it is so important in developing a flower garden that you dig in your organic material when digging the plot. This allows the nutrients time to work. Nitrogen fertilisers include dried blood and soot. Phosphate fertilisers include bonemeal and steamed bone flour – this is the residue left behind after the gelatine and fat have

Giant pansy, lamb's tongue, evening primrose, fescue.

been taken out in the glue factory. Potash fertilisers include wood ashes which are sprinkled over the surface or forked in. Beware! Do not try and substitute coal ash which contains a host of materials that are toxic to plants and could destroy a good deal of time and effort.

Pests and diseases

Too many people give too little attention to ridding themselves of pests and diseases and merely spend a lot of money on the wrong treatment. This way they don't cure the problem, lose money and end up wrongly blaming the manufacturer.

The first priority in tackling disorders is to have dug in plenty of humus. When soil content is high in humus the plants get all the nourishment and moisture they need and problems are less likely to occur.

The second priority is to see that you are vigilant in checking your plants. Catching problems early enables you to tackle them better. Early detection, rapid identification and quick treatment will stop the spread of problems which could, if left, lead to considerable loss.

The third important factor to bear in mind is not to use anything to treat your problems that will damage or even kill the important garden predators which do your plot so much good.

These predators include insect-eating birds, hoverflies, ladybirds, spiders and even hedgehogs. Absence of any or all of these can allow pests to intrude. When dealing with insects, bear in mind that they can be divided into two main groups from a gardener's point of view – those that bite, which eat the leaf, stem and shoot, and those that suck, which attack the sap inside the leaf stem. From this it obviously follows that there is very little point in attacking sucking insects with a poison sprayed on the outside of the leaf. But this is what considerable numbers of gardeners do. For the suckers there are contact sprays which can also be effective in dealing with biting insects. There are two main, non-poisonous types – derris and pyrethrum extract.

CUT FLOWERS

The moment that you take a knife or a pair of scissors to a flower in the garden you condemn it to slow but certain death. Those bought from the shop will already have been undergoing this process for some hours, if not days.

You can do nothing to stop this but what you can do is prolong the life of the flowers.

Picking

When picking flowers it is best to do so in calm weather. Cool, cloudy days are best. Always remember that a flower deprived of water will wilt far quicker when it is picked. If picking for arrangements then do so some time before you intend to use them so that they can be conditioned (see Preparing and conditioning). On hot days try and collect them early in the morning before the sun is high so that plants can still benefit from the cool of the night and have their food reserves intact.

Selecting your flowers is very important. Always look at them carefully before cutting, choosing flowers at the right stage of their life cycle. Many plants, for instance roses, peonies, irises and shrub flowers, are best cut as the buds begin to unfold. Others, like chrysanthemum and dahlias, need to be in full bloom. Make sure that you cut the flowers cleanly rather than pulling or plucking. A clean cut not only means that your stems will take up water more easily, but that you protect the parent plant from damage. Stub scissors (see Equipment) are best.

When cutting flowers in the garden take with you a container of water so that your flowers spend as little time as possible out of water. Cut a good length of stem and, where possible, cut at an angle so that you are exposing as large an area as possible to the water. This will also mean that the stems do not sit squarely on the bottom of any container which could impede the absorption of water. As you cut, strip away any unwanted foliage. If you are cutting a lot of flowers place the container of water in the shade to avoid wilting.

Preparing and conditioning

As a general rule place all picked flowers immediately in a container of luke warm water which allows the full stem to be covered. If you are planning to use the foliage then that, too, can be covered, but make sure that any flower heads remain above the level of the water. Tough and woody-stemmed plants like roses, chrysanthemums and carnations may benefit from a soaking in even warmer, but not hot, water.

If your flowers have been out of water for any time, re-cut them at an angle before placing them in the water. Those flowers with tough stems will also need their ends crushed. They will ooze a milky, sticky fluid and should be stood in boiling water for 30 seconds to break the seal formed by this fluid which hardens on meeting the air. Peel off any bark before crushing the ends.

If your plants have especially floppy stems they can be held rigid, while standing in water, by wrapping them in stiff paper. Hollow-stemmed plants can have their life prolonged by filling the stems with water. Turn them upside down, gently trickling the water in. Plug the ends with cotton wool.

Equipment

While vast numbers of vases and complicated equipment are not necessary for displaying and arranging flowers, some basic equipment will help to do the job properly and show off your blooms to their best advantage. The best type of scissors are called 'stub' scissors which have a specially serrated edge which allows you better to cut tough stems and wire.

In order to anchor your flowers properly in a vase you will need a variety of materials. *Florists wire* – also known as stub wire – and silver reel wire are the main types used. Stub wire helps to strengthen or replace stems, while silver reel wire binds wired flowers to each other. Fuse wire can be used for this. In addition,

some three-layered chicken wire can be used to anchor flowers. Make sure it is wide enough to take several stems through each hole. Make sure, that it is firm and well-placed otherwise the flowers will slide about in the vase and this could both ruin the arrangement and possibly topple over the vase.

Tall, bulky flowers may need some extra ballast. Try a small bag of sand on top of the wire or the florists foam.

Foam. Florist's foam is a dense, sponge-like material that can be bought in square or round-shaped blocks and cut to size. It is often called by the most common brand-name – Oasis. It is used to support the stems of a plant in a display. Soak the foam in water for about an hour and then simply slot in the stems of the flowers. Most stems will slide in easily but with those that are too delicate you may have to make your own holes with a skewer or something similar. When cutting the foam to size you should make sure that it will fit into the container leaving enough room at the sides so that extra water can be added daily to keep the foam moist. The foam can be re-used several times.

Watering can. For topping up the water you will need a small watering can with a long, narrow spout that will allow you to pour water into the vase without disturbing the flowers.

These items are used for flower arranging: pin holders, green foam, candelabra, pruning scissors, wire cutter and a flower knife. Also shown is wide and narrow tape, very useful and sometimes indispensable for making bouquets, corsages and buttonholes.

Pin holders. These are very useful for supporting all sorts of flower displays. They come in a variety of forms and are made of metal or plastic. They can be bought in an unobtrusive green colour so they don't show. The flower stems are simply pushed down onto the numerous fine prongs embedded in the base.

Tape. Some flower arrangements will need masking tape as an additional form of support, criss-crossed over the rim of a container or as a way of concealing wiring. It can also be used when taping flowers for bouquets or buttonholes.

Simply wind tape around the stems. It is sometimes called gutta-percha.

Clay. Adhesive clay, often-known as Oasis-Fix, is used for anchoring unstable container arrangements. It can also be used for securing foam or a pinholder to the bottom of your container.

Disguises. There is also a variety of disguises that can be used to mask the use of anchorage materials. These can be bought from a good florist or collected yourself in the garden, woods or even at the sea-side. Choose materials that will look attractive with your display, won't smell offensive and which will last.

Containers. The container that you select for an arrangement has obviously got to suit the flowers and the style of your arrangement and generally the fewer flowers you are using, the more important becomes your choice of container.

Flower vases have been made in Europe for over 200 years but in all this time not one shape has emerged as the 'classic'. This is because, whether it is a teapot with the lid missing or a fine cut-glass vase, the container can look right if the arrangement and the flowers are suitable. What is critical, then, is the relationship between the container and the flowers. Too many flowers for a small vase or too few in a big one, flowers that are too tall for a short vase, or too short for a tall one – all this can harm the overall effect that you are seeking to achieve.

Shape is also important and so, too, is colour. A whole variety of containers, not all of them designed for flowers, can come to your aid in displaying your blooms.

A porcelain cake-stand, a round cake-tin painted and filled with water, old gravy or sauce boats, an old glass scent bottle or ink-well or even that old china tea-pot ... all these and more can be put into use. Nowadays, of course, there is a vast range of containers specifically manufactured for flower arrangements, from the tall, thick glass ones with holes in them to the delightful creations of the Wedgewood and Sykes companies.

Any deep dish or shallow urn raised on a stem makes arranging easy and has the added advantage that it lifts the flowers up and gives them a more elegant look.

Crystal and glass vases are splendid for an arrangement which is light and attractive and which, when placed with a shaft of light on it, creates an ethereal effect. To help promote this look the water must be perfectly clean and a little drop of household bleach will help to keep the water in glass vases clear.

Experience has shown that flowers tend to last longer in metal vases. While the reason for this remains unclear it may have something to do with the fact that it keeps them cooler. Bronze, copper or brass are all ideal.

You may only have a handful of flowers but they can be enhanced by the colour of the container. Blue and orange crocuses in a black jug or bright yellow daffodils in a yellow glass vase will show what we mean.

White is perhaps the commonest colour for vases having the virtue that its clean simplicity goes well with most flowers – soft or strong.

Cleaning vases can be a problem especially with long or

narrow necked types. Try using old newspapers lightly rolled and inserted into the vase when it is three-quarters full of water. Allow this to stand for an hour or so and then shake firmly, swishing the water around. Other materials that can work on stubborn marks include sand or tea-leaves.

Porcelain vases tend to accumulate a build-up of dirt and will benefit from a periodic soaking in really hot, soapy water. But first, make sure that the vase is not even slightly cracked or the hot water may finish it off.

If you use metal containers like brass, copper or silver they can be kept clean with a regular rinse under the tap.

Flower arranging

The art of flower arranging goes back centuries. In eastern countries like Japan it is considered one of the finest social skills and, although a good deal of time and training can go into it, the oriental style of flower arranging can be stunningly simple. In other countries vast swathes of flowers and foliage are assembled bursting with colour and scent. But whatever the style and the size one thing unites all forms of flower arranging – the simple idea that if you are going to take a knife to fresh flowers there is an obligation to invest a little time and effort to see that they are well displayed.

If you enjoy cut flowers then you will enjoy them all the better if you think about the colours, the shape of the vase, the addition of a little foliage to set off the flowers.

Once you would have been obliged to choose your flowers and your arrangements according to the season, but the speed of world transport, the advent of hot-house cultivation and the development of new, hardier flowers means that even if you can't grow them there may well be a bountiful supply of all sorts of flowers available in your local florist's shop. You will, however, have to pay quite a steep price for the privilege of displaying out of season flowers. When planning an arrangement always try to ensure that it fits into the general scheme of the room. Don't let it mask a picture on the wall behind it or so dominate a dinner table that the guests have to bob up and down in their seats to talk.

Method. Your approach to arranging will have to vary according to the type of container but there are some basic ground rules which should be observed.

A sense of proportion is, perhaps, the most important factor in a successful arrangement. The aim is to achieve a balance of colour, shape and size.

Unless you are decorating a church hall or a really grand dinner or ball, it is probably best to keep the flowers you use as natural as possible.

As a general rule try and follow these basic steps. First try and define the outline of your arrangement, then add the major blooms and leaves to the centre of it, only then working outwards to fill out the whole arrangement. Keep the whole display flowing and gradually leaning forward. Avoid the temptation to overcrowd the display.

Do not cross stems and try to keep the main mass of the arrangement at the base. Finally, avoid a clash of colours – and that doesn't simply mean obviously unsympathetic clashes but putting hot colours like orange with cool colours like pale green.

As we have said, the style of your arrangement will vary

according to the size and shape of the container. With a tall, upright vase the tallest stem will generally be the most important. If it should slip or move about it will destroy the rest of the display. Make sure that it is fixed correctly. The arrangement should generally be about twice the height, certainly no more, of the container. The width should be about the same as the height. This will contrive to give your arrangement a balanced shape and form.

To avoid an effect that is too symmetrical, place the stem slightly off-centre, to the right or the left.

Once you have defined your outline shape with the foliage and flower sprays, add a focal point to your display. Try open roses, dahlias or chrysanthemums which tend to draw the eye to them. Place two or three stems so that they rise well over the rim of the vase. Then place another two further back to intensify the effect. Experience will show you that the colour you place at the centre of your arrangement will tend to dominate even though you may only use a few flowers.

Place all stems so that they incline towards the middle – even ones which are sloping forwards as well. Don't cut the stems too short and take them to the vase before cutting so that you can better gauge the length. Ensure that all the stems are below the water line.

Arrangements by colour. In addition to arranging your flowers so that the colours go together sympathetically, you can also make arrangements of same-coloured flowers. Here are some ideas.

Yellow. Flower arrangements in yellow give the room a marvellous sunny, summery feel and can be used to brighten up both the decor and the spirits ... even in the depths of winter.

If your shop can provide you with foreign grown or hot-house supplies, or if you gather early flowering varieties like winter aconites or daffodils, you can cheer up the spirits when it is still cold and gloomy outside. The range of shades between the bright gleaming buttercup yellow and the delicate pale yellow of the primrose gives the arranger plenty of scope.

Try any of the following: snapdragon, lilies like 'Destiny' and 'Charity', yellow roses like 'Goldilocks' and 'Allgold', wallflowers, tulips, primulas, pansies and lupins. Flowering shrubs like broom, honeysuckle and azalea can be used to give a depth and variety to the arrangement. You can also use winter jasmin, golden rod, marigold, witch-hazel and chrysanthemum. Try broom with yellow tulips and white lilac or honeysuckle with winter jasmin and yellow roses.

Red. For the purposes of this section we will assume that red embraces all hues from pink to crimson... and what a variety this gives the arranger. When one thinks of red flowers the mind turns, perhaps automatically, to roses and the pages of any good catalogue will list a bewildering array of shades, sizes and varieties. Here are just a few ideas.

For a deep, dark-red rose try 'Garnet'. 'Anne Poulsen' lightens just a shade, while for a strong, sturdy deep pink try 'Queen Elizabeth'. For a subtle salmon pink select 'Betty Uprichard'. The great concert hall singer 'Kathleen Ferrier' gave her name to a rose of a striking cerise pink.

In addition to roses, however, there are a host of other flowers that will make your red arrangement striking or subtle, dominating or discreetly colourful.

Try clematis (mauve/pink), geranium (all shades), dahlias, geums, zinnias, snapdragon, pansy, pinks, red-hot poker, hydrangea, phlox, Canterbury bells and peonies.

Blue. As a colour, blue is somewhat cold. It does not have the fire of red or the cheerfulness of yellow. On its own it can tend to be a little lifeless – though having said that, the first sight of bluebells in spring is a sign of regeneration and of optimism. However, blues will usually need a contrasting colour to really set them off and this can be provided with other flowers or by the use of a contrasting container or background. Blue shows up best against yellow, pale green or white. Whatever you do don't put it against a dark background.

Here is just a short list of some blue flowers you may care to use. Delphiniums, bluebells, cornflowers, love-in-a-mist, hydrangea, hyacinth, iris, larkspur, scabious, clematis, and veronica.

Green. Arrangements in green may, at first sight, seem a little odd since most foliage is also green, but such is the range and variety of green material that subtlety and flair can create a magnificent arrangement with almost nothing else. It has the added advantage that the passing seasons are of little or no significance in the making of green arrangements, since every garden should boast greenery whatever the time of year.

When employing green the secret is to look for subtle contrasts in colour and shape, in texture, and size. Try the rounded shape of angelica with the thin, dark foliage of a helleborus foetides. Green arrangements look cool, especially in the summer, and will often last two or three weeks as long as they are kept watered. To get an idea of the range of shade and shape here is a list. Camellia (light green leaves and sprays), rue (blue-green foliage), rosemary (silver-green leaves and stem), privet (dark-green foliage), fennel (soft-green foliage and stem), angelica (soft-green seed heads), eucalyptus (dark green leaves), variegated peri-winkle (dark-green foliage), euphorbia (green flowers).

Wiring. While flower arrange-ments in containers can look as natural as you like, those which are made to be worn or held have usually to be con-structed on some form of wir-ing and may well look a little unnatural.

The better the wiring, howev-er, the more likely it is that you will manage to make your bouquet, your buttonhole or your posy look natural.

One of the simplest methods of wiring, and one which can also be used in some container arrangements, is simply to push some of your stub wire as far as possible up the stem of a heavy-headed flower. Hollow-stemmed, thick-centred flow-ers can also be strengthened with stub wire by bending one end into a hook and inserting the wire down through the centre of the flower head. Push right into the stem, embedding the hook in the flower itself.

Flowers with other types of stems will need to be wired externally. This applies espe-cially to those that are very delicate, brittle or damaged in any way. To create a look which is as natural as possible leave about 2 inches of stem. With a strong, firm stem you can simply insert the wire up through the stem into the flower head. For those with more delicate stems insert the wire sideways through the base of the flower head, pull it through and then bend the wires down either side, paral-lel with the stem, and then twist them in wide loops around the stem before bin-ding with tape.

When the whole stem is going to be discarded a system of cross-wiring is employed. This technique is most commonly used in bouquets with pinks and carnations. Push two light wires at right angles through the base of the flower head, bend them down and twist them together, to form a false stem.

There is another wiring meth-od which comes in handy, particularly for foliage, flowers that are too fragile to be pierced or with especially large bouquets. With this method you don't insert the wire into the flower. One end of the wire is bent into a hook, about one inch long, which is placed flush up against the top of the stem just below the flower head. The other end of the wire is then brought up and twisted round and around the hook end, continuing down the stem before being taped. There is a variety of other techniques for supporting and assembling foliage and flowers and you will, no doubt, invent your own. The secret is to start with an unambitious assembly and practice before attempting something you intend to wear – or give to others to wear.

There is a variety of different arrangements that are either worn or carried.

A corsage is a bouquet of flowers which is usually worn, or fixed to a ribbon, for a wedding or some other important occasion. When starting to make a corsage it would be as well to start small. Begin with something that will not take too long and wear it or carry it for a while to see how well it survives the experience, and if it needs any improvements in design or support. You may find that it is unbalanced or out of proportion.

A bouquet is usually carried, again for weddings and other important occasions. The secret with a bouquet lies in skilful and unobtrusive wiring. It should have a focal point but, and this should be an advantage, unlike a vase arrangement the flowers can be arranged at any angle.

Do not overload your bouquet because it is already having to bear the weight of the wires and other mounting materials and this may place too much strain on the whole assembly.

Where possible try to mount more than one flower on a piece of wire to economise on wire and reduce the overall weight. Frequently a bud and leaf, one laid on the other, will form the tip of a spray and can be mounted on one wire. All stem wires can be wound together and taped.

With large bouquets it can sometimes be a good idea to make them in two or three sections then bring them together for final binding.

A less ambitious alternative is to make a single bouquet with one large, perfectly-formed bloom and some dressing materials.

Posies. These are small bouquets of flowers usually made up of clearly defined bands of colour massed around a central flower, which is usually a rose-bud but can be almost anything that is rounded. Usually the posy is shaped in a conical manner rather like an upturned saucer. Stems of the flowers are gathered at the back, wired and bound with a handle of material to make them easier and more comfortable to hold.

Buttonholes. With these the important thing is to make sure you have selected suitable flowers – ones which won't get in the way or flop about. Attach any foliage, like fern, to the main bloom with some fine wire then cover with tape and bind a safety pin along the stem so that it can be pinned to the clothes.

DRIED FLOWERS

Dried and preserved flowers may be no substitute for the beauty and fragrance of fresh cut flowers but they have a good many uses and also the advantages of not wilting and of being available all the year round.

They can be displayed in a whole host of ways since they do not need to stand in water. Many can even be preserved for their smell as well as their looks. Roses and pinks are among many varieties that will retain most of the appeal of fresh cut blooms ... if treated properly. They are splendid in making pot pourris, filling sachets, sweet bags and pillows.

When picking ensure that both the flowers and the foliage are in good condition. They should be fully-grown but not past their best. Flowers that are picked too early may be too limp to preserve properly while those that are picked too late may be going to seed.

The best time to pick is at midday after the dew of the morning has dried out. Do not pick if it has been raining. Any moisture in your flowers will attract mildew.

Almost every flower can be preserved in one way or another and our guide here is merely an indication of what treatment best suits what type of flower. Obviously, we could not include every flower, so the guide simply covers a range of the more common

Many garden plants can be dried (Statice suworowii).

ones to give you a good idea. Experiment yourself with a variety of flowers starting with the easiest technique of air drying and working your way up. Most flowers will need to be wired before drying if you intend to retain the stem because once dried it becomes brittle and crumbly. This process is explained later in this section.

The traditional drying tech-

Cut flowers, often very expensive, last much longer if you dry them. Take care that you buy fresh ones.

niques are air drying, water drying (yes, really), and powder drying. A variety of materials are used in this latter process like borax, sand, and silica gel and glycerine.

In addition to these drying techniques you can also simply press your flowers.

Air drying

This is the simplest method and all that is really needed is a cool, dry, airy place which is preferably dark. Most flowers with strong stems are ideal for this method but softer-stemmed flowers may shrivel or become to brittle and need to be wired (see page 36). Gather your flowers in small bunches of the same variety. Strip off the leaves and tie them near the end of the stem. Make sure your flower-heads are not too bunched or air will not be able to circulate around them. Tie gently but tightly enough to stop the stems slipping out once they begin to dry. Hang them upside down, from a line or other support, in your airing spot. Drying upside down ensures that the stems do not bend and that the flower heads keep their shape. This process will take at least one week for even the most delicate of flowers to dry properly. Larger, more sturdy flowers which contain more moisture, could need as much as three weeks. They are properly dry when they feel papery to the touch.

With plants that are dried especially for the scent, and also with some annuals and perennials dried for the colour, it may be better to dry quickly in hot air. Put them in an airing cupboard spread on a piece of chicken wire or something similar that has many holes in it. Rest the heads of the flowers on top of the wire with the stems hanging through. This process should take only a few days.

Many flowers with distinct attractive smells, which you intend to use for pot pourris, pillows, etcetera can be similarly dried but pluck the petals and leaves that you intend to use first and scatter them on a wire tray.

Water drying

Unlikely though this sounds as a method for drying flowers, most shrubby plants and those which have tough stems are best dried by this method. Pick the flowers as they are beginning to dry anyway. Insert them in about 0.5 inch of water and leave them until all this has been absorbed.

Powder drying

This method is best suited to large single blooms or fragile heads. When using it make sure you always dry the same type of flowers together since the drying times will vary according to flower and type. The process uses what are called desiccants which are drying agents. There are a number of these but the ones explained here can all be simply dried and re-used.

The most commonly used desiccants are *borax* and *alum* – usually employed mixed together in equal amounts because the borax may stick to the dried flowes if used by itself. Both are relatively inexpensive powders and are fine and light so will only support the more delicate of blooms. Using these the flowers should take about one to two weeks to dry.

Sand or *silica gel*. When you need a heavy desiccant, which will support sturdier blooms, these can be used. Sand is the heaviest and also the slowest of desiccants and will usually take two or more weeks to work. It is best to use clean, sharp sand and it would be wise first of all to wash it in a bucket skimming off any dirt.

Dry in the oven before using. Silica gel, also available from chemists, is best used for stronger plants. It is rather more expensive than other desiccants but it is quicker and this gives you the benefit of preserving the flower rather closer to its original colour. It should take as little as 3-6 days.

Glycerine. This preserves rather than dries the plants and works by keeping them constantly moist and supple as opposed to a drying agent which removes all moisture. It is probably best suited to foliage but also works well with some seed heads and one or two flowers. Experiment to find out which it suits best.

If drying the foliage and the leaves, clean and pare away any bark from the stems and split them.

Immerse in water for two or three hours and then place the stems in a mixture of one part glycerine to two parts very hot water to a depth of 4 inches. Leave in a cool, dark place until all the glycerine mixture has been taken up and the leaves have turned colour. It may be necessary to add a little more solution if it has all been absorbed before an even colour has been achieved. Light foliage should take one to three weeks.

Using desiccants. Pour your powder into an airtight container or old cake tin or sandwich box – whatever is used it is imperative that it should form a tight seal when closed. Pour to a depth of 1 inch and gently place the flower heads on top of the layer of powder making sure they do not touch each other. Then trickle a coating of powder over each bloom making sure they are all covered. With flowers that have a lot of crevices you may need to use a stick or needle to separate the petals because it is vital that each bloom gets a very thorough coating. Continue pouring so that each bloom is well covered and then seal and place the container in a warm, dry place.

Wiring before drying

Most dried plants have stems that become brittle and can simply crumble away on handling unless you have wired them before the drying process. Attempting to wire afterwards would be extremely difficult so don't risk damaging them for the sake of a little extra precautionary work.

Buy some 20 gauge florist's wire and some florist's adhesive tape which is usually available in different colours. Carefully push the wire up the centre of the stem as far as it will go, feeling it up the stem with your fingers. When the flower head can no longer flop over, stop and dry. When dried you can conceal the wire with the tape.

If you are wiring the flower head only, simply cut off the

stem so that only an inch or so remains and then push the wire up through the base of the flower. This method has an added advantage in that the wire will insert easily into a base of foam or chicken wire for arrangement purposes.

Preserving the scent

Since the beginning of time flowers have been gathered and used fresh and preserved for their fragrances, and there are a number of ways of prolonging the fragrance so that you can enjoy it longer.

Among the most popular are pot pourris, scented pillows and cushions.

Pot pourris. Some people will have heard of elaborate and expensive methods of making pot pourris and will, as a consequence, have been put off the idea of making them.

In fact, the process can be simple, enjoyable and highly rewarding.

There are many sweet-scented flowers growing in the spring that are ideal for gathering and making into pot pourris. Violets, lilies-of-the-valley, wallflowers, narcissi and azaleas all fall into this category. As your garden gradually bursts into life, almost any favourite sweet-smelling flowers can be used. Freesias, roses, pinks, mock orange and the scented leaves of pelargoniums are among those that are ideal.

The range of flowers that you can use will probably mean that you never make the same pot pourri twice.

When making your pot pourri it will be necessary to 'fix' the fragrance and these 'fixatives' vary. The best type to use is one that will both do the job that is asked of it and, at the same time, add some perfume of its own. Try citrus peel. Orange, lemon or tangerine peel pared and dried slowly in a cool oven and then ground in an electric blender. Another common fixative is ground orris root.

Oils and spices are also needed to retain and enhance the fragrance of your flowers. The commonest oils used include lavender oil and rose oil, although you can buy special pot pourri oils.

Spices used include cloves, cinnamon, nutmeg, coriander and allspice. Mix these together in advance so they are ready to use. As a rough guide, when mixing use one tablespoon of each of the spices to two tablespoons of the fixative.

The easiest pot pourris to make are dry ones. Take a selection of fragrant roses, lavender, carnations and other flowers that retain their scent after drying. Add other petals for their colour when dry, delphiniums, cornflowers and marigolds for example, and then make a thin layer of the petals and aromatic leaves on a wire rack in your airing cupboard. In one or two weeks they should become crisp and dry. Take a quart of the dried flowers and petals and 2 oz of your spice mixture, add a few drops of oil and shake thoroughly. You can do this in a plastic bag. Leave tightly closed for about three weeks by which time the pot pourri mixture should be ready.

Place in a pomander, in china or metal pots, in an open bowl or in brandy-style balloon glasses. Keep them out of direct sunlight.

You can also make a moist pot pourri that lasts much longer, although it also takes longer to mature.

Mix equal quantities of partly-dried flowers like carnations, lily-of-the-valley, mock orange, roses, violets and make up to one gallon.

Add 1.5 oz of orris root powder, a couple of drops of oil and half a tablespoon each of crushed cinnamon, cloves and nutmeg. Mix well and put a two inch layer in the bottom of a glass jar. Sprinkle over it a thin layer of salt and repeat the layers until the jar is full. Seal and leave for at least one month stirring frequently. When ready place in your pots.

Scented bags or pillows. Use a natural fibre like muslin, cheesecloth, lawn or voile that will allow the scent to penetrate. Cut out two pieces of fabric to the size you need, sew double seams round three sides and turn inside out.

Fill the bags with your mixture and sew up. For a rose pillow try a mixture of one pint of rose petals, 1 oz of powdered cloves and one ounce of powdered mace.

Arranging dried flowers.
There are many advantages in making arrangements of dried flowers. They can be as colourful, often as fragrant and almost always easier to handle than fresh cut flowers. In addition to this, they are obviously going to last longer which means you don't have to keep making new arrangements. Use plenty of flowers so that you create an abundant, massed effect while at the same time hiding the stalks. Dried flower arrangements will be much lighter than cut flower ones since you are not using a bowl or vase of water, so you will need to fill the bottom of your container with stones or sand to weight it down. Place your florist's foam on top of this, packing it in tight. The general effect given by an arrangement of dried flowers is much more muted than with cut flowes. Browns, blues and yellows tend to predominate but in pastel shades rather than bold bright ones. Remember, when arranging, that you can use almost any foliage... and you should not restrict the arrangement to flowers. Try seedheads, grasses, leaves etc. A typical dried flower arrangement might include yellow and brown achillea, delphiniums, larkspur, rose-hips, love-in-a-mist, hydrangeas,

Dried flowers can be made into beautiful bouquets.

A decoration that will last for a very long time.

water reeds, ferns and grasses. Most of the deep colours will come from the garden, with delphiniums and larkspur being among the most common and prettiest. Delphiniums give all shades of blue, while larkspur gives mauves, purples, pinks and white. Lamb's ear (stachys lanata) has soft-grey leaves and purple flowers; hollyhock (Althea) is valuable for its spikes in bud that give your arrangement a really dramatic appeal; seed heads like those of the poppy, broom and marigold are also important since they, too, give some variety to the arrangement. Thistles will add another dimension, setting off the other flowers. The list is endless and one of the most enjoyable aspects of drying flowers is making your own decisions about what you like, what dries well and what looks good in your own arrangements.

Pressing.

To satisfactorily press flowers you will have to restrict your ambitions to those that are generally fairly small, flat and delicate. Larger flowers do not press well unless you break them up into individual florets, press them and then re-assemble later. Do not try pressing flowers with hard or fleshy centres.

Pick plants for pressing on dry days and at a time when they are at their best. You are planning to keep them, so why not choose a perfect specimen. ·Pick in mid-morning or mid-afternoon. Moist flowers may well go mouldy in your press. Do not try to press flowers that are going to seed, or damaged flowers.

Most flowers will not retain their original colour very well when pressed, fading slowly over a period of time. However, this effect can be minimised. It is often caused because moisture has been retained when they are pressed, so they should be dried as much as possible straight after picking.

Method. Arrange the plants for pressing into groups so that thick, thin, foliage and flowers are pressed in groups. This ensures that similar thicknesses are pressed together. Cut away any thick stems and press down any awkwardly-shaped leaves. Use a fine paintbrush and blunt tweezers as much as possible to avoid handling them.

To press, arrange the flowers on a small sheet of blotting paper making sure they are not touching. Some plants may have retained moisture, so one day after putting them into the press – or between heavy books – check to see if the blotting paper is at all damp. If it is then change the paper. Repeat until it no longer shows any signs of dampness otherwise you will get mould on your flowers. As soon as they are properly dry you can increase the pressure by tightening the wing-nuts on the press to the full pressure or by adding more heavy books. If you are away from home or do not have a press or heavy books to hand you can just as easily do this in a magazine, transferring the flowers to the press when you return home. You will discover which plants are best for pressing but a list of the best would have to include: maple, chamomile, pot marigold, clematis, larkspur, blue-bell, snowdrop, winter-flowering jasmine, forget-me-not, daffodil, peony, poppy, pelargonium, primrose, buttercup, golden rod, clover and pansy.

Dried flowers
The following flowers are quite suitable to be dried.

Achillea filipendulina - yarrow
Alchemilla mollis - lady's mantle
Allium giganteum - onion flower
Amaranthus caudatus - love-lies-bleeding
Ammobium alatum - sand flower
Anaphalis margaritacea - pearl everlasting
Artemisia ludoviciana - white sage
Astilbe - false goat's beard
Astrantia major - masterwort
Celosia argentea - cockscomb
Centaurea - cornflower
Cynara scolymus - globe artichoke
Delphinium
Dianthus barbatus - Sweet William

Dipsacus
Echinops - globe thistle
Eryngium alpinum - sea holly
Gysophila - baby's breath
Helichrysum - everlasting
Helipterum - immortelle
Hydrangea macrophylla
Lavendula officinalis - lavender
Limonium sinuatum - sea lavender
Lunaria annua - honesty
Molucella laevis - bells of Ireland
Physalis - Chinese lantern
Protea - honeypot sugerbush
Solidago - golden rod

Flower	When to pick	What to pick	Method
Anemone	spring, summer, autumn	flowers	powder drying
Azalea	late spring	flowers	powder drying
Camellia	late spring	flowers, foliage	glycerine
Clematis	spring, summer, autumn	flowers, seedheads	air drying, glycerine (seedheads)
Convallaria	summer	foliage	air drying, glycerine, water drying
Daffodil	spring	flowers	powder drying
Dahlia	summer	flowers	powder drying
Delphinium	summer, autumn	flowers, seedheads	air drying, powder drying
Dianthus	summer	flowers	powder drying
Forsythia	spring	flowers	powder drying
Helleborus	winter	flowers, foliage	glycerine
Helichrysum	summer	flowers	air drying
Hyacinth	spring	flowers	powder drying
Hydrangea	late summer	flowers	glycerine, water drying
Iris	spring	seedheads	air drying
Narcissus	spring	flowers	powder drying
Peony	summer	flowers, foliage	glycerine
Primula	spring	flowers	powder drying
Rose	summer	flowers, foliage	glycerine
Tulip	spring	flowers, seedheads	glycerine (seedheads)
Viola	spring, summer	flowers	powder drying

WILD FLOWERS

Our wild flowers are rapidly disappearing and all gardeners with a true feeling for plants can help to keep them alive by growing at least one or two in their own gaden.

This does not mean, however, roaming the countryside and pulling up wild flowers. The first law of the Countryside Code beseeches all true nature lovers: 'do not pick the flowers – leave them for others to enjoy'. Few enough have survived the ravages of the modern world where the farmer's tractor, the motorway builder and the spread of towns and villages has ripped up important countryside sanctuaries for both wild flowers and animals.

By growing wild flowers in our gardens we not only preserve our flora and bring a bit of the real countryside into them, but we also help to provide a habitat for butterflies and bees – both of which are finding it harder and harder to find suitable food.

So how do we go about bringing wild flowers into our garden?

First of all, since almost all wild flowers are readily grown from seed and are native to our climate and soil conditions, they will grow very easily. It is not necessary to raid the countryside since most can be obtained from specialist growers and seedsmen. But they can also be collected in seed form from wild plants where they are abundant.

Cowslip, forget-me-not, mullein, foxglove, elecampane and cornflower, to mention but a few, set seed in abundance and a few seed pods, judiciously snipped off, will not go amiss. More and more people are discovering that there is something truly rewarding about cultivating a natural wild flower section in their garden. While there is obvious delight in a neat, well-ordered flower border there is also tremendous pleasure to be derived from setting aside a quiet corner of the garden and turning it over to wild flowers. There is something almost magical about a wild corner and you may well find that it is to this spot that you turn more and more for pleasure. In this well-ordered life there is something quite inspiring about a bit of wild beauty.

Farming methods these days have all but doomed the pasture and copse to those few areas protected by governments. However, we all have a chance to create our own wild flower garden – albeit in a modest fashion.

Here is a guide to some tall, medium and small-growing wild flowers that will add a touch of romance and mystery to some quiet corner of the garden. Alternatively they can be grown in a conventional flower border.

Tall. Willow herb (Epilobium angustifolium) is a dramatic perennial, growing to 4 feet with spikes of bright purple flowers in June to October. Motherwort (Leonorus cardiaca) grows to 4 feet and has pale mauve flowers from July to September. In olden days its leaves were boiled with honey and taken to relieve heart palpitations.

Mallows like the common mallow (Malva sylvestris) are rampant plants which will often seed themselves and spread all over the garden. Its roots go so deep that if it is not dug up regularly it may be hard to remove. Nevertheless, grown carefully it is a magnificent plant, reaching 4 feet and bearing pinky-mauve cup-shaped flowers from June to October.

Mullein (Verbascum thapsis) is another splendid wild flower growing to 6 feet in a single season and bearing striking, towering spikes of rich yellow flowers. A tea made from the flowers is good for hacking coughs.

Giant bellflower (Campanula latifolia) reaches 5 feet, has large, copious blooms of blue, bell-shaped flowers in July to October.

Elecampane (Inula helenium) is probably the largest of all the native plants but, sadly, it is very rare in the countryside. Rather like a small, hairy sunflower, it grows to 5 feet and has golden, rayed flowers which can measure as much as 3 inches across.

Sea holly (Eryngium maritimum) grows to 3 feet with spikey, holly-like leaves and sky-blue flowers.

Hemp agrimony (Eupatorium cannabinum) thrives in damp spots but will grow in any moisture retaining soil. It bears pale, lilac flowers from July to September.

Melitot (Melitotus officinalis) grows to 7 feet with yellow, trumpet-shaped flowers which are borne from July to September.

There are countless more tall-growing flowers and these include a vast family of wild roses like the dog rose (Rosa canina), the burnet rose (Rosa pimpinellifolia), the downy rose (Rosa tomentosa) and the delightful sweet briar (Rosa rubiginosa).

Medium. One of the delightful things about wild flowers is that so many of them have common names that hint broadly at a use to which they were put many, many years ago.

Sneezewort (Achillea ptarmica) was said to make one sneeze a great deal after just one sniff. It grows to 2 feet with clusters of white flowers, which often used to be put in bridal posies, and blooms in June and July. It is a member of the yarrow family whose commonest member (Achillea millefolium) grows to 2 feet with white or pink flowers from June to September. Both have the virtue of being able to last a long time in flower arrangements. Cut and dry and use in long-lasting arrangements and they will retain their beauty until Christmas.

Wood betony (Stachys betonica) is a hairy perennial growing to 1.5 feet high with purple flowers in July and August. It is very popular with bees.

Sweet rocket (Hesperis matronalis) grows to 3 feet with purple, white flowers that smell of violets.

Common agrimony (Agrimonia eupatoria) is a delightful plant growing to 2 feet with spikes of perfect yellow flowers in June to August.

Soapwort (Saponaria officinalis) is so called because it is a natural detergent. It has charming, pinkish-white flowers borne from July to September and grows to 2 feet.

Lady's smock (Cardamine pratensis) grows to 1.5 feet and has mauve flowers which are borne in May to mid-July. Also called cuckoo flower because its flowers arrive with the cuckoo.

Field scabious (Scabiosa arvensis) grows up to 3 feet with tightly-packed florets of lilac blooms and a perfume that

attracts swarms of bees and butterflies. It blooms in July to September. Canterbury bell (Campanula medium) grows to 2 feet in a bushy form and bears large, bell-shaped flowers of blue, pinks and white in June.

Hound's tongue (Cynoglossum officinalis) grows to 2 feet with grey-green lance-shaped leaves which are said to resemble hound's tongues. It bears maroon coloured flowers in June to September.

Small. Thrift (Armeria maritima) has tiny round mauve flowers that grow to about 9 inches and bloom in May to September.

Pasque flower (Pulsatilla vulgaris) is one of the most beautiful of all wild flowers. It grows to about 5 inches with rich purple-coloured flowers shaded pink on the reverse. It flowers from Easter to May which is why it is also sometimes called the Easter flower. That popular border plant the Bellis has a wild, double form. (Bellis perennis) which comes into bloom in March, at a time when few other flowers are around. It blooms in shades of pink, scarlet and crimson.

Meadow cranesbill (Geranium pratense) grows to about 1.5 feet with bright blue flowers in June to September. There is a whole family of other cranesbills that makes a delightful show in a wild garden. Blood cranesbill (G. sanguineum) has crimson flowers in July to August. Hedgerow cranesbill (G. pyranaicum) has rose flowers from June to August. Shining cranesbill (G. lucidium) has pink/white flowers from May to August. Wood cranesbill (G. sylvaticum) has rose flowers in June and July.

Herb Robert (G. robertianum) comes from the same family. It has pink five-petalled flowers in May to September and a long-beaked seed case. It gives off a strong smell which accounts for its old nick-name 'Stinking Bob'.

Lungwort (Pulmonaria officinalis) is a hardy, herbaceous perennial used centuries ago as a medicinal herb but which is ideal as a border plant. It has purple/blue flowers in April and May.

The list is endless and you can have a lot of fun discovering your own favourite wild flow-

ers and planning them into your special wild garden. It is possible to grow wild flowers that will be in bloom all year round. From March to September the range is enormous. Here are a few ideas for the less abundant months.

January. Winter aconite (Eranthis hyemalis), Christmas rose (Helleborus niger), lesser periwinkle (Vinca minor).

February, snowdrop (Galanthus nivalis).

October. Giant bellflower (Campanula latifolia), autumn crocus (Crocus nudiflorus), cornish heather (Erica vulgaris), pink oxalis (Oxalis floribunda).

November. Strawberry tree (Arbutus unedo), great mullein (Verbascum thapsus), meadow saffron (Colchicum autumnale), bellis (Bellis perennis).

December. Christmas rose (Helleborus niger).

Grasses No wild garden would be complete without a variety of plants to cover the bare earth and keep down weed Grasses do this very effectively and there are endless varieties. Blue-eyed grass (Sisyrinchium augustifolium) grows to 1 feet in hardy clumps with star-shaped violet flowers in May to October.

Feather grass (Stipa barbata) is a compact, tufty grass growing to 2 feet with long plumes of a light biscuit colour in June and August. These are ideal for drying and using in winter decoration.

Hare's tail grass (Lagurus oratus) is an ornamental grass often grown solely for its decorative qualities. It reaches one foot with hairy, grey-green leaves and slender stems which terminate in fluffy white ovoid flowers from June to September.

Other ideal ground cover plants also offer decorative uses both inside the garden and in arrangements.

Dwarf comfrey (Symphytum grandiflorum) is a splendid weed suppressor and forms a dense carpet of green leaves and sends up 6 in. orange-tipped bells. A member of the borage family (Borago laxiflora) has green, hairy leaves and stems with turquoise flowers which resemble little pointed bells. It spreads very fast.

Lenten rose (Helleborus orientalis) will allow little to grow under its spreading palmate leaves and also bears splendid speckled bowls of flowers in apple-blossom, peach blossom, claret and dove purple.

There are plenty more. Once again, seek out your own favourites but be sure that you know all their properties – good and bad – before you introduce them into your garden. Some will spread rapidly, others will put down deep roots.

Weeds are frowned upon by the modern gardener. The very word is derogatory. But there are very many so-called weeds that not only look attractive but have a good many uses.

Most gardeners would be unwise to introduce invasive weeds into their garden deliberately, but some will find their way in anyway. Here are some of the more colourful and useful: coltsfoot with highly decorative foliage like small, velvety water lilies. It grows on poor soil where almost nothing else will. It has miniature golden flowers in the spring, and possesses many curative powers. Beware, however, of its creeping roots.

Daisy. Hated by those gardeners who prize above all things a neat, well manicured lawn, the daisy nevertheless is a highly attractive addition to any wild garden. Its seeds don't spread widely like many so-called weeds because they are not fluffy and thus are not carried far in the wind.

Dandelion. Who hasn't, as a child, blown the seeds of the dandelion off its stem in billows of white tufts? It provides rich pollen food for bees and, again, is attractive and useful in a wild garden. Beware, however, because it gives off ethylene gas which will impede the growth of nearby plants and can cause pygmy fruit.

Potentilla. The most common wild potentillas are the silverweed and the cinquefoil. Both are lovely wild plants that do not deserve the title of weed.

Silverweed (Potentilla an-
serina) has lovely decorative
leaves which are ideal for
arrangements and long-
stalked yellow flowers.
Cinquefoil (Potentilla rep-
tans) has rich green long
leaves and honey-coloured
flowers. Beware, however,
because one plant is capable of
colonising as much as 12
square yards in one season.

As we have already said, no
wild flowers should be uproot-
ed in their natural state. But
that is not to say that you cannot take seeds from plants in
the wild as long as you are very
careful how you go about it.
These can then be propagated
in the same way you would
any normal seed. Indeed, this
can be of positive benefit to the
wild plants themselves because, by removing one or two
seed capsules, you can prolong
the life of a good many wild
perennials. They will no longer have to waste energy producing too much seed.
Take a pair of sharp, pointed
scissors and cut off the whole
stalk – this avoids any pulling
or loosening of the mother
plant. Do this on a dry day so
that the seed capsule is not
damp.
Dry the capsules in an airy
room spread out on sheets of
brown paper. To be fully dried
they will need as much as ten
days. Squeeze the seeds out of
the capsules when fully dry
and place them in little enve-
lopes or matchboxes to await

sowing. Make sure that you
have clearly marked which are
which so you know what you
are sowing when the time
comes.
As a general rule most wild
plants will have ripened their
seeds about two months after
they have finished flowering.
In any case, collect the seeds
before the winter rains come.
Spring flowering plants ripen
their seeds by mid-summer
and are best sown as soon as
they have been harvested – in
early July onwards – so that
they have a chance to get
themselves well-established
before the arrival of winter.
The same applies to biennials,
which are sown in July to
bloom the following year.
Annuals should be kept until
the following year and sown
first in a cold frame early in the
new year, or in open ground in
the flowering site in April.
When sowing, use a proper
sowing compost. Sow thinly
and cover only lightly with a
layer of compost. Water gently
and then cover with a sheet of
glass or polythene in the way
you would when germinating
any normal seed.
At the two leaf stage – when
the seedlings have grown two
pairs of leaves – replant in
trays, spaced at one inch intervals.
Allow them to become established before planting out into
the growing site.
It should be abundantly clear
that, since Mother Nature
manages to do all this without

such an elaborate procedure, merely scattering the seeds in your garden could achieve some results. However, nature's way is very wasteful of seeds. This method not only saves on seeds but makes sure we produce strong, healthy plants with few of the failures that happen with random sowing.

Some wild plants, however, are best raised by sowing directly into the soil in the flowering site and this includes most annuals and biennials. Scatter the seed in circles and rake them into the surface of the soil.

Most wild flowers can be increased by division and, in any case, it is probably a good idea to lift wild flowers every four or five years to ensure that root spread isn't getting out of hand and to divide the clumps.

Once they have stopped flowering use a fork to lift them gently out of the soil and knock off the loose earth. Gently divide the clumps in the way you would any normal garden plant, making sure that each offset comes with some roots. Some wild flowers are better suited to certain locations or uses in the garden and here is a list of flowers and some ideas for their location.

Water gardens.

Water lilies – (Nymphaea alba) white flowers in July and August or (Nupharlutea) yellow flowers June to September.

Water violet (Hottonia palusris) pink flowers May and June.

Bogbean – (Menyanthes trifoliata) white and pink flowers May and June.

False bullrush – (Typha latifolia) dark brown spikes.

Flowering rush – (Butomus umbellatus) pink flowers July to September

Rock garden.

Birdseye primula – (Primula farinosa) pink flowers May and June.

Spring squill – (Scilla verna) blue flowers April and May.

Winter aconite – (Eranthis hyemalis) yellow flowers January to March.

Maiden pink – (Dianthus deltoides) pink flowers June to September.

Pink oxalis – (Oxalis floribunda) pink flowers May to October.

103
FLOWERS

On the following 33 pages you will find detailed descriptions of some 100 varieties of flowers. For each variety you will find information about the care they require, about available colours, about the natural flowering period (often different or shorter than in a greenhouse) and about the time of year when they are available in the shops.

A large number of the cut flower varieties described are suitable for your own garden. Nothing is as nice as a garden from which you can, during the greater part of the year, pick flowers with which to brighten up your home: tulips, narcissi and forsythia in spring; sweet william, cornflowers, foxgloves and marigolds in summer; dahlias, chrysanthemums and asters at the approach of autumn. Remember though that the flowers that bloom just one season or part of a season in your own garden, are often available in the shops for much longer; sometimes all year round. These days it seems that nearly all plants can be brought to flower under glass to decorate every conceivable occasion. So you can always go to the better florists for roses, carnations, chrysanthemums and gerberas, etc. Not all the flowers described here can be grown in your own garden. For some a greenhouse is necessary, and sometimes the required climatic conditions are such that it is better to leave their cultivation to the professional grower. For instance, flowers that come originally from the tropics can only be grown here for an acceptable price under glass when large areas are planted at the same time. If, as an amateur, you have already been able to achieve the necessary soil temperature, air temperature and humidity in your own greenhouse, it will still seem an extremely expensive hobby to cultivate similar flowers. Thanks to the advanced growing techniques and good distribution, a wide assortment of cut flowers is available these days at an affordable price all year round. This book will form a guide: to show you the possibilities and limitations, and to give you ideas.

ACACIA dealbata
Mimosa

Flowering period: December to March.
Colour: Yellow.
Care: Acacia dealbata is a small tree or bush which you can plant in greenhouse border or, to restrict size, in 3 inch pots. Move the plant gradually into 12 inch pots or small tubs. In winter the minimum temperature should be 4°C and if early-flowering 7°C. In summer Acacia dealbata can stay outdoors in a sheltered spot. In winter it needs a cool, but frost-proof spot. Allow plenty of light throughout the year and supply the plants with water freely in spring and summer and modestly at other times.
In shops: Spring and winter.

ACHILLEA filipendulina
Yarrow

Flowering period: July to September.
Colour: Lemon-yellow.
Care: The filipendulina is a border species of yarrow. It is a beautiful plant which has mid-green leaves and grows to a height and spread of 3-4 feet. The flowers are yellow and belong to the umbellife-rae. Plant between October and March in any well-drained garden soil and in a sunny spot. In Novem-ber cut it back to ground level. The filipendulina can be propagated by division or by seed in a cold frame during March.
In shops: Summer, autumn.

ACONITUM napellus
Monkshood

Flowering period: July and August.
Colour: Violet-blue.
Care: Aconitum is a herbaceous perennial growing to approximately 3.5 feet. The flowers grow in clusters and can be dried easily. Plant between October and March in partial shade in deeply-dug, moist soil. It will grow in full sun but only if it is kept moist. Mulch the plants annually in spring and cut back after flowering to encourage further stem growth. In October the flowering stems will have to be cut down. Propagate by division in October or March.
In shops: Late summer and autumn.

AGAPANTHUS campanulatus
African Lily

Flowering period: Late summer.
Colour: Pale blue.
Care: Agapanthus is a hardy deciduous plant, grown in clumps, which carries crowded umbels of flowers, loses its leaves in winter and has fleshy roots. It will thrive in any well-drained soil in a sunny sheltered spot. Plant outdoors in mid-April and be careful to set the crowns 2 inches below soil level. Agapanthus needs a lot of water in the growing season and less in winter. Cut the stems back to ground level after flowering. In frost pockets protect with bracken or sand October to April. Propagate by division.
In shops: June-October.

ALCHEMILLA mollis
Lady's mantle

Flowering period: June to August.
Colour: Yellow.
Care: The Alchemilla or Lady's mantle is a hardy, herbaceous perennial which grows to a height of 18 inches and develops light-green hairy leaves. It has a yellow outer covering instead of petals. The flowers of this plant can be dried. Plant between October and March in a sunny spot or in partial shade in moist well-drained soil. It will need twiggy sticks for support. Cut back the flowering stems to a height of 1 inch after flowering. You can propagate this plant by division.
In shops: Autumn.

ALLIUM giganteum
Onion flower

Flowering period: June.
Colour: Lilac.
Care: The Allium giganteum is a hardy bulbous plant producing large star-shaped umbels which are 4 inches wide. It grows up to 4 feet high. It will grow best in the sun and a well-drained soil. It is possible to dry the flowers of the Allium. Plant in September to October covering the bulbs to three times their own depth. It may need staking. Dead-head the flowers and remove stems and leaves in autumn. It may be necessary to divide the clumps when they become so thick it stifles flowering.
In shops: April-November.

ALSTROEMERIA aurantiaca
Peruvian lily

Flowering period: June to September.
Colour: Yellow to orange.
Care: The Alstroemeria is the hardiest in a family of fifty herbaceous perennials originally coming from South-America, which have fleshy tuberous roots and thin leaves. It can be grown outside, unlike many of its relatives, and is highly-prized by growers for its striking trumpet-shaped flowers which grow up to two inches wide and come in a rich yellow to orange colour, often veined in red. It grows to a height of 3 feet. Good garden varieties include the beautiful 'Dover Orange' and 'Lutea'. Plant young, pot-grown specimens in March or early April. While planting, make sure that you do not disturb the delicate roots. Plant Alstroemeria 15 inches apart, in groups, to a depth of about 5 inches, in well-drained soil.
Problems are to be expected when the soil stays moist for too long. The plants prefer a sheltered spot. You may find that no top growth is made in the first year. Support the specimens with twiggy sticks, especially when you plant the Alstroemeria in an open spot in your garden.
You can also plant in autumn, but cover the plants in that case to protect them from frost. Once Alstroemeria has survived the first winter, there will be no problems during the next frost-periods.
Unless you are growing for the seeds you will need to dead-head the plants. Cut the stems down to ground level in autumn once the leaves have died.
Propagate by sowing seeds in March in pots of seed compost or in a cold frame. Prick out seedlings into pots that are 3.5 inches wide. Plant out into the flowering site the following spring.
Alstroemeria can also be propagated by dividing established clumps into 6 inch clusters in March or early April, replanting them straight-away without removing any of the soil. You can also remove individual roots in March or April and pot them in 6 inch pots. Plant on into peat in a cold frame and plant in permanent site a year later.
Early growth in the Peruvian lily can be badly affected by slugs which may eat young shoots. Swift moth caterpillars can also cause damage by feeding on the roots. Plants can be stunted by virus disease which shows as yellow mottling.
In shops: All year round.

AMARANTHUS caudatus
Love-lies-bleeding

Flowering period: July to October.
Colour: Crimson.
Care: The Amaranthus is the most popular specimen of this species of half-hardy annuals. It is grown mainly for its beautiful, 18 inches long drooping racemes of flowers, which can be dried easily. The stems of this plant turn crimson in autumn. Plant in deeply-dug and cultivated soil which has been well-manured. The Amaranthus likes a sunny spot though this variety will grow well in partial shade and less good soil. Plant out in May. Can also be grown in 5 inch pots at 15°C.
In shops: Mid-summer until autumn.

AMARYLLIS belladonna
Amaryllis

Flowering period: September-October.
Colour: White, pink, yellow.
Care: Amaryllis is a bulb plant, native to South Africa (where it flowers between March and August). The plant carries 6-12 flowers on one stem. The leaves develop in early summer and die-off before the flower forms. The Amaryllis should be treated as a pot plant: winters in a cold, frost free greenhouse; summers complete with pot outside. The bulbs can be left in the ground for several years. Propagate by young bulbs or seed.
In shops: March-April, August-October.

ANAPHALIS margaritacea
Pearl everlasting

Flowering period: August.
Colour: Pearly white.
Care: A hardy herbaceous perennial which grows to about 18 inches with tapering grey-green leaves and pearly white flowers. Plant between September and April in well-drained soil and in a sunny spot. Anaphalis will also grow in the shade, if you choose a dry spot. Cut back hard in the autumn if it becomes untidy. Propagate by division between September and April, or by basal shoot cuttings 2-3 inches long, taken in April or May. Allow these shoot cuttings to take root in peat and sand (equal parts).
In shops: Summer.

ANEMONE coronaria
Anemone

Flowering period: March and April.
Colour: White, blue or red.
Care: A spring-flowering hardy herbaceous perennial growing to 12 inches. The Anemone grows in well-drained, good soil in a sunny spot or partially in the shade. Plant at a depth of 2 inches in September or October. Successive planting means that this specimen can be flowering almost all year round. Large corms will take up to three months to flower while smaller ones take up to six months. For winter flowering protect the plants with cloches from October onward.
In shops: January-August.

ANTHEMIS
Camomile

Flowering period: June-September.
Colour: White or yellow petals, yellow stamen.
Care: Anthemis is a family of annual, biennial and perennial herbs, which are easy to propagate from seed. The best known is Anthemis nobile (Roman camomile), which is used as a herbal remedy. Among the prettiest is Anthemis bierbersteiniana, 0.5-1 foot tall. Good as cutting flowers are Anthemis tinctoria (yellow camomile), 1-2 feet tall, and the similar Anthemis sancti-johannis, 1 foot tall.
In shops: Autumn.

ANTHURIUM andreanum
Flamingo plant, Painter's palette

Flowering period: May to September.
Colour: Red and white.
Care: The Anthurium is an evergreen greenhouse plant. Its flowers are very attractive, they have a large fly-leaf with the actual flowers inside it. It requires plenty of warmth and a humid atmosphere. They do best when the temperature is kept constant and the minimum winter temperature should be at least 13°C. Ideally it should be 16°C. Pot in March in 3 parts peat to one (by volume) sphagnum moss. Water from October to March. Provide the plant with liquid feed from May to August.
In shops: All year round.

ANTIRRHINUM majus
Snapdragon

Flowering period: July to frosts.
Colour: Various colours, yellow, white, red, orange.
Care: Antirrhinum is a specimen that shows a variety of forms growing as high as 4 feet. They are easy plants, for they grow in any well-cultivated garden soil enriched with manure. Plant up to 18 inches apart. Stake the tall varieties. To be sure of prolonged flowering you must remove the faded spikes. Set out young plants in September for early-summer flowers. Keep them in a cold frame during winter. Antirrhinum can be grown as pot plants under glass at 7°C for winter flowering.
In shops: Late summer, autumn.

ARTEMISIA ludoviciana
White sage

Flowering period: July-September.
Colour: Grown for silver foliage.
Care: Artemisia or White sage is a hardy herbaceous perennial which produces tiny, button-shaped yellow flowers which are all but insignificant. Grown especially for its splendid silver-grey, aromatic feathery foliage, which can be well used in arranging flowers. It will thrive in light, well-drained soil. Plant in October and March in full sun. Cut the stems back almost to ground level in October.
In shops: Not commonly sold.

ARUM italicum
Arum

Flowering period: September to November.
Colour: Cream-white.
Care: Arum is a warm border bulb which is best-suited to south- or west-facing walls. It has cream-white spathes and is free-fruiting. Its berries are beautiful and can be kept for a long time in water. The leaves are used to make bouquets. Arum is planted in autumn in moist, but well-drained soil. They can be grown in a sunny or partially shaded spot. Arum increases freely by producing plenty of seeds.
In shops: Autumn and early winter.

ASCLEPIAS tuberosa
Milkweed

Flowering period: July and August.
Colour: Bright orange.
Care: The Asclepias is a hardy herbaceous perennial ideal for a wild garden. It grows up to 2 feet. The flowers grow in little clusters. Plant Asclepias in a sunny but moist position during the months October and March. It likes deep, sandy and peaty soil with no lime. It may need staking. Sow seeds under glass in March at 15°C. Prick out and harden off April/May. Asclepias needs a lot of water. Provide plenty when the summer is dry.
In shops: Late summer/autumn.

ASTER
Aster

Flowering period: Dependent on type: May-June or August-November.
Colour: Blue, pink, red, white.
Care: Aster is a herb-like plant family of about 250 varieties. Most important for cultivation are the autumn flowering Aster novi-belgii and the Aster novae-angliae, both of which come from North America. The cut flower varieties are hybrids of these types. Autumn asters need a sunny or partially shaded spot. To prevent them running wild, they must be split every 2 or 3 years.
In shops: August-October.

ASTILBE
False goat's beard

Flowering period: June to August.
Colour: White, pink, red.
Care: Astilbe is a variety of hardy perennial from the Saxifrage family. The flowers can be dried. They like permanently moist soil and thrive in sun or shady spots. Plant the False goat's beard in October to March and be sure to water the plants freely when it is a hot and dry summer.
Astilbe needs cutting down to ground level in October and should be lifted every three years. Divide and replant in March or April.
In shops: Late summer/autumn.

ASTRANTIA major
Masterwort

Flowering period: June and July.
Colour: Greenish pink.
Care: A hardy herbaceous perennial growing to 2 feet and bearing star-like flowers which measure about 1 inch across. The flowers can be dried. Plant between October and March in ordinary garden soil. Chose a spot that provides partial shade. The plant may need some kind if support if it is exposed. Cut down the stems in late summer. Propagate by division between October and March.
In shops: Early/mid autumn.

BANKSIA
Banksia

Flowering period: Dependent on type.
Colour: Several shades of yellow.
Care: Banksia is a member of the Proteaceae family. A woody plant, it comes from Australia and New Guinea. It puts forth cob-shaped blooms containing countless flowers. The family consists of about 50 varieties. Of these, the Banksia australis is the most commonly sold in the shops.
In shops: All year.

BOUVARDIA x domestica
Bouvardia

Flowering period: June to November.
Colour: Pink, white or red.
Care: Bouvardia is a greenhouse, evergreen shrub with fragrant flowers which are produced over a long time. The plants need a light, sunny spot and a high humidity. Pot the plants in March in 6 inch pots. Maintain a summer and winter temperature of 13°C. Bouvardia needs a period of rest in winter to start flowering again. Stop established plants twice, between April and the end of March. Keep the temperature at 5-10°C, be sparing with water. From May to September water well and feed.
In shops: May-December.

CALENDULA officinalis
Marigold

Flowering period: May to frosts.
Colour: Orange or yellow.
Care: The Marigold is a hardy annual with a bushy habit, it flowers longer than most. It will thrive in poor soils and under the worst conditions. Best results, however, will be obtained when you use well-drained soil. If you grow the Marigold for cutting, be sure to pinch out terminal buds to encourage laterals. Dead-heading prolongs the flowering. September sowings flower in winter under glass.
In shops: Summer.

CALLICARPA bodinieri
Beauty berry

Flowering period: July.
Colour: Pink.
Care: Callicarpa or Beauty berry is a deciduous
shrub which is really grown for its profusion of red to
purple berries which follow the flowers. The flowers
are pink and the shrub looses its leaves in winter. It
is rarely cultivated and can be grown outdoors only
in mild areas. Plant under glass in pots at a temperature of 4°C. Put a few plants together to obtain good
fruiting. Or in mild areas outside in October to March
in good soil, and a sunny spot. A south wall is
prefered.
In shops: Spring and autumn.

CAMPANULA medium
Canterbury bell

Flowering period: May to July.
Colour: White, blue, pink or violet.
Care: A biennial popular for use in flower borders.
The Campanula has green, hairy leaves and an
upright habit. The plant thrives in any well-drained
soil in a sunny spot or partial shade. Plant this
specimen in September to April. It grows up to 3 feet
and therefore may need staking. Remove the faded
flower spikes. The Canterbury bell can be flowered in
pots under glass. Pot them in September. Let the
plants overwinter in a cold frame and move them to a
greenhouse in February at a temperature of 10°C.
In shops: Late spring, early summer.

CALLISTEPHUS chinesis
China aster

Flowering period: July to frosts.
Colour: Pink, red, purple, white.
Care: Originally the Callistephus was a dark purple
flower, but it has been superseded by varieties that
flower from July right up until the first frost periods
and which come in the above colours. The flowers
will provide lovely bouquets which will last for a long
time in a vase. Popular as border plants there are a
number of recommended varieties which include
Bouquet Powder Puffs, Chrysanthemum Flowered
Mixed, Pinnochio Mixed and Pompon Mixed. All are
erect plants growing to about 18 inches and bearing
mid-green coarsely-toothed leaves. The flowers are
similar to daisies, but differ in form and colour. To
prevent wilting do not grow China asters in the same
ground in two consecutive years. The China aster
prefers a medium loam soil, though you should get
reasonable results in any good garden soil.
Plant the specimens in an open, sunny position and
make sure that the tall varieties get some good
protection from the wind. These varieties may require
some staking.
Sow seeds under glass in March at a temperature of
16°C, then transplant them into boxes, let the plants
grow on and finally harden off in a cold frame before
planting out in May. Plants from a late sowing in May
or June can be potted and grown in frames during the
summer and, if you have one at your disposal, be
flowered in frost-free greenhouses from October to
December. In that case you can use the flowers for
arranging in winter.
If the China asters do not get enough light (for
example because they are planted too close
together), or if they are given too much water or
nitrogen, they may wither. This can also happen
when you do not harden off young plants well
enough. China asters may be attacked by aphids
when they are young. Caterpillars can threaten the
stems and leaves. Various diseases that can be a
threat to them include Tomato Spotted Wilt Virus,
Cucumber Mosaic Virus and Callistephus Wilt, the
latter even taking its name from the plant.
In shops: Summer/early autumn.

CELOSIA argentea (cristata)
Cockscomb

Flowering period: July to September.
Colour: Red, orange, yellow.
Care: The Celosia argentea is a dwarf, compact plant with crested flower heads. They can be grown outdoors as well as indoors. The plants need a rich, well-drained soil and a sheltered, sunny spot in the garden. If you grow the Celosia under glass, maintain a temperature of 16°C. In this case they need good ventilation and regular watering. Do not plant the Celosia outdoors before the flowering starts. Harden off the plants before planting in May. The flowers can be dried.
In shops: March-December.

CENTAUREA
Cornflower

Flowering period: June to October.
Colour: Pink, red, white, blue, yellow.
Care: There are some 500 varieties of Centaurea, both annual and perennial. The annuals Centaurea cyanus, Centaurea moschata var. imperialis and the winter hard Centaurea macrocephala are particularly good cut flowers. All of these can grow to a height of 3 feet. The shorter, more bushy types are suitable as border or pot plants. Remove dead blooms to encourage others to flower. All varieties can be sown in April or May. Propagation is possible by division.
In shops: Summer.

CHEIRANTHUS cheiri
Wallflower

Flowering period: April to June.
Colour: Yellow.
Care: The Cheiranthus or Wallflower is a hardy, sub-shrubby perennial usually short-lived but with freely produced flowers. The plant grows up to 2 feet. Numerous varieties of this specimen are available in colours which also include white, orange, scarlet. Sow the Cheiranthus in May or June and plant them out in October, in well-drained soil and sunny spot. Pinch out the tips of the plant when it is 5-6 inches high to encourage branching.
In shops: Late spring early summer.

CHELONE obliqua
Turtle-head

Flowering period: August and September.
Colour: Deep pink.
Care: A hardy, herbaceous perennial which grows up to 2 feet. Special are its leaves that have prominent veining and its flowers, born in terminal spikes. Sow in April or May, plant them out in a seed-bed and let the plants overwinter there. Plant between September and March in a sunny or part-shaded spot and deep, light soil. It is necessary to cut down the dead stems in October. Propagation by division in September to March.
In shops: Autumn.

CHRYSANTHEMUM
Chrysanthemum

The Chrysanthemum is an enormously versatile garden plant. If you grow it in clumps it will look splendid. You can also grow it by itself and, equally, it will shine. This plant also has the great advantage that, because there are so many varieties, you can grow them from the end of July to the end of October and thus, have a splendid spread of magnificent cut flowers for your home. They are among the finest of cut flowers because they last so much longer than many others and, in a cool atmosphere, with the water changed regularly, should last as long as two weeks.

They always have composite flowers, which means that one flower actually contains many little flowers. The family itself contains up to two hundred species of hardy annuals, hardy and half-hardy sub-shrubs and herbaceous and greenhouse perennials. There are so many types and varieties, however, that the real problem lies in selecting which Chrysanthemum you are going to grow.

In the alpine Chrysanthemum you have a variety which bears neat little white flowers with yellow centres rather like a daisy. The annual species are all free-flowering and hardy.

The carinatum is perhaps the most spectacular. Try 'Merry Mixed' or 'Monarch Court Jesters'. The perennials can be distinguished because they have ovate, deeply lobed foliage. Perhaps the most commonly-grown of these is the Maximum. Try 'Wirral Pride'.

The fourth group of Chrysanthemums, and the one most prized for its blooms, is the so-called 'Florists' Chrysanthemum. This is a vast group of border perennials and hardy greenhouse plants which fit into seven sub-groups. Incurved, Reflexed, Intermediate, Single, Anemone Centred, Pompons, and other types.

Even within these groups the size of bloom and flowering time varies so much that proper classification requires them to be further broken down into categories. But good examples of each would be: Incurved, 'John Hughes'; Reflexed, 'Plush Red'; Intermediate, 'Yellow Fred Shoesmith'; Single, 'Mason's Bronze'; Anemone Centred, 'Thora'; Pompons, 'Fairie'.

Soil preparation is very important with Chrysanthemums. If it is possible, be sure to double dig the plot, breaking up the bottom of the trench and digging good, farmyard manure into the top spit. Add bone meal or hoof and horn at the rate of 2 oz to the square yard. Some varieties will suffer if you leave them in the ground in winter, so study the growing hints on the seed packet you buy. Lift the roots of the Chrysanthemum in November if you are intending to save them over winter. Place the roots in good soil in a cold frame with the minimum of water to prevent the delicate roots from drying out. Ventilate well in all but frosty weather. Plant the little Chrysanthemums out of doors the following spring, thinning the basal shoots if they are in profusion since this could make the plant weak.

Propagation of the Chrysanthemum can be done by division, but most commonly this is achieved by taking cuttings. For this cutting select strong basal shoots that are about 2.5 inches long and take them off in February, making a clean cut immediately below the node. Plants that you grow in the open air can also be transferred into pots or tubs for the winter. To be sure the plants survive this small operation, soak the soil around the roots thoroughly a day before lifting the plants. Be extremely careful not to damage the roots when you are lifting them. Originally the Chrysanthemum flowers in autumn, but today this fine cut flower is available throughout the year. Often the professional nursery-men use greenhouses where circumstances can be kept ideal so that they can have flowers on the market all year round. Commercially, the flowering of many Chrysanthemums can be advanced or delayed by controlling the amount of light they are given in electrically-lit greenhouses.

In shops: All year round.

CLARKIA elegans
Clarkia

Flowering period: July to September.
Colour: Various colours.
Care: The Clarkia elegans is a hardy annual which
has an erect growth and is ideal for a border plant.
You can also use it as a cut flower or pot plant. It
grows up to 2 feet and bears double flowers up to 2
inches across on spikes which can be up to 12
inches. It likes a medium to light soil and a sunny
spot. Heavy feeding will delay the flowering. Sow
seeds in March, thinning or planting out to required
spacing.
In shops: Summer and autumn.

CONVALLARIA majalis
Lily-of-the-valley

Flowering period: April and May.
Colour: White.
Care: The famous Lily-of-the-valley is a rapid-
growing plant which is grown from a rhizome,
flowers in the spring and likes moist soil and a
partially shaded spot. The little white flowers spread
a delicious scent, the plants grow best under trees or
bushes. Once common in the wild it is now less so. It
can grows up to 8 inches and spreads up to 2 feet.
Plant crowns singly in September or October about 4
inches apart. Top dress in winter with leaf mould or
compost. Propagate by division.
In shops: All year round.

COREOPSIS tinctoria
Coreopsis

Flowering period: July to September.
Colour: Bright yellow.
Care: Coreopsis tinctoria is a hardy annual, growing
to 3 feet. It has dark green stiff stems and a profusion
of flowers which are 2 inches across. They are free-
flowering, bushy plants, and they should thrive in
any good well-drained garden soil. Tall plants will
need staking. If you leave these plants undisturbed,
you will find that they seed freely in the surrounding
soil. Sow seeds in the period March to June.
In shops: Summer and autumn.

COSMOS bipinnatus
Cosmea

Flowering period: August to September.
Colour: White, crimson, rose.
Care: This plant is a half-hardy annual growing up
to 3 feet. It prefers a light, even poor soil and does
best in very good hot seasons. When it has reached
its full height it will need staking. To ensure a good
succession of flowers it is advisable to dead-head
regularly. To assure yourself of plants that flower in
summertime you can sow them in April under glass.
Plant out the specimens in May.
In shops: Summer to early autumn.

CROCOSMIA x crocosmiiflora
Crocosmia

Flowering period: July to September.
Colour: Yellow to red.
Care: Crocosmia is a bulb from the tropics grown from small corms which produce sword-shaped green leaves and which grow up to 2 feet in height. They need open, sandy, well-drained soil on an open spot and copious amounts of water in summer. Plant Crocosmia 6 inches apart and 3 inches deep, in clumps on the south side of a sheltering wall. When it turns cold again in October, lift the corms.
In shops: June-October.

CYCLAMEN coum
Cyclamen

Flowering period: December to March.
Colour: Pink, carmine, white.
Care: The Cyclamen is a very well known tuberous plant found wild in Mediterranean countries. It grows up to 4 inches, is hardy and bears flowers 0.75 inch long on pointed buds. All cyclamens thrive in well-drained soil enriched with organic matter, and in a cool, lightly shaded spot. Shade the plants from the sun and shelter them from wind. Plant the Cyclamen in late summer and early autumn in clusters which are 6 inches apart.
In shops: All year round.

CYNARA scolymus
Globe artichoke

Flowering period: Autumn.
Colour: Purple.
Care: The Globe artichoke is a perennial mainly grown as a vegetable (the heart of the flower is a delicacy), but which is attractive enough to be grown by many as an herbaceous plant. Grow the Cynara in a sheltered, sunny spot in fertile soil which has been well-dug and enriched with rotted manure. Propagate by detaching rooted suckers in April or November. Pot, overwinter and plant out. You can also sow the Cynara under glass, pot them, harden them off and plant them outdoors in June.
In shops: Summer, autumn.

DAHLIA variabilis
Dahlia

Flowering period: Mid-July to September.
Colour: All colours.
Care: All modern Dahlias, which come in numerous forms, sizes and colours, derive from this species. They are not hardy and top growth will be hit by the first frosts. Start from tubers in warmth in February or take new cuttings when 3 inches long. These cuttings, however, are extremely delicate. Plant out tubers or cuttings from the end of May in well-dug enriched soil. You can also plant the tubers outdoors directly in April. Cut when two-thirds open. Tall varieties need staking.
In shops: Summer, early autumn.

DELPHINIUM
Delphinium

Flowering period: June to August.
Colour: Blue, purple, white, pink.
Care: The Delphinium is an erect-growing, hardy annual reaching a height of 4 feet, with a spread of 16 inches. The plants will flower the same year from seeds sown under glass in February. Plant the specimen out in September to March in deep, rich soil in a sunny, well sheltered spot. Flowers that grow too high you should stake in April. After the flowering cut back the stems to nearest healthy leaf below the raceme. Cut back to ground in autumn.
In shops: Summer.

DIANTHUS
Pinks, carnations

This is a genus that contains annuals, perennials and evergreen plants used in gardens as well as in the professional nursery of cut flowers. It includes the popular pinks, carnations, and sweet williams.
Old fashioned pinks grow up to 15 inches and flower in June. Popular varieties of these pinks include the 'Charles Musgrave' (white and green) and the 'Inchmery' (pale pink).
Modern pinks grow to a height of 15 inches and they all come from a hybrid which has been produced by crossing an old-fashioned pink with a perpetual-flowering carnation. They are faster-growing, they produce many more blooms in June and July and will usually flower again in September and October. Both types are grown in well-dug soil enriched with manure and dressed with bone meal just before setting out the plants in March or from September to November.
Border carnations grow to 3 feet. They are hardy perennials and flower once from July to August. Annual carnations grow to 18 inches, they are not suitable for cold areas and flower from July to autumn frost. Both are grown in the same soil as described before for pinks. Plant perennials in March or in September and October. Annuals you can plant in May.
Perpetual flowering carnations are grown as greenhouse perennials to be sure there is an all-year cut flower available. A good supply of winter blooms at 7°C. Prolific production at 9°C. Start your plants or rooted cuttings in pots in the months February or March. Pot them on. Stop young plants when they have six or seven pairs of leaves. Feed after the first buds appear. Damp down staging when the weather is hot.
In shops: All year round.

DIPSACUS
Dipsacus

Flowering period: July.
Colour: Lilac.
Care: Dipsacus is a biennial from which, in earlier times, wool was carded from the overblown flower heads. Nowadays, these are used in dried bouquets. Sow out in June in a moist, shady spot. Thin out and transplant to final spot in September at 1.5 feet intervals. Protect against frost. For strong growth a well-drained, lime rich soil is necessary. The plants reach a height of 3-7 feet.
In shops: Summer, early autumn.

DORONICUM
Leopard's Bane

Flowering period: April to June.
Colour: Golden yellow.
Care: The Leopard's Bane is a splendid, early-flowering hardy herbaceous perennial which, if you dead-head the plant regularly, will produce a second flower-show in autumn. Plant the Doronicum in October to March in deep, moist soil and choose a sunny or partially sunny spot. Some plants may need staking. Cut down the stems to ground level in autumn. Propagate by division between October and March.
In shops: Summer.

ECHINOPS
Globe thistle

Flowering period: July and August.
Colour: steel-blue.
Care: The Echinops or Globe thistle is a hardy, herbaceous perennial which bears an impressive spherical cluster of beautiful blue flowers which can be cut and dried for winter decoration. Plant these specimens in October to March in well-drained soil and a sunny spot. Cut the stems of the plants to ground level in October. Propagate them by division in suitable weather between October and March.
In shops: Autumn.

EREMURUS robustus
Foxtail Lily

Flowering period: May and June.
Colour: Yellow.
Care: This so-called Foxtail Lily is a hardy herbaceous perennial, significant for its impressive spikes of flowers, which grows up to 10 feet. The spikes themselves may grow to 2 feet. Plant these perennials in September to October placing the crowns 4 feet apart and 6 inches deep. The Foxtail Lily needs well-drained soil and a sunny spot in the garden. Mulch the flowers annually. Propagate by division in September or October.
In shops: Summer.

ERIGERON
Fleabane

Flowering period: July and August.
Colour: Blue/purple.
Care: This splendid garden plant is a hardy herbaceous perennial with a striking bloom with narrow rays of colour spreading out from a yellowish-golden centre. Plant October to March in moist, well-drained soil and make sure it is in a sunny spot. If you dead-head the flowers it will encourage flowering later in the season. Cut the stems down to ground level in autumn. Propagate by division between October and March.
In shops: Autumn.

ERYNGIUM alpinum
Sea holly

Flowering period: July to September.
Colour: Blue.
Care: The Sea holly is a striking hardy border plant, which grows to 2 feet with steely-blue flower heads which are surrounded by prominent steely-blue spiked leaves. Plant this specimen between October and April in any ordinary well-drained soil and a sunny spot in your garden. Cut back the stems of the plant to almost ground level after flowering.
Propagate by division and plant the little plants out in March.
In shops: Autumn.

ESCHSCHOLZIA californica
Californian poppy

Flowering period: June to October.
Colour: Orange – yellow.
Care: The Californian poppy is a magnificently-coloured hardy annual which grows to 15 inches, and which produces 4 inches seed pods after flowering. This plant likes poor, sandy soil and plenty of sun. If you remove seed pods you will stimulate more flowers. If the Californian poppy is sown in September it will need cloches to overwinter. For cutting gather the flowers at bud stage. Sow seeds, September to March directly on the spot, they don't survive planting out.
In shops: Summer and early autumn.

EUPHORBIA fulgens
Spurge

Flowering period: October-March.
Colour: Orange, red, white, pink.
Care: The Euphorbia fulgens is a native of Mexico. The plant owes its attractiveness to the originally orange coloured crown-like leafy tendrils. It is grown here as a greenhouse cut flower, in a temperature of 18-20°C. After cutting, the stems should be kept in water at 80-90°C for a short while to prevent loss of the milky sap. Room temperature should be no lower than 15°C, otherwise the stems will droop.
In shops: Nearly all year round.

FILIPENDULA
Meadow sweet

Flowering period: June-July.
Colour: White, pink, red.
Care: Filipendula is a family of fairly tall perennial herbs. They need a moist shady spot. The flowers grow in plumes, with their lower shoots longer than those at the top. Most suitable as a cutting flower is Filipendula purpurea, up to 3 feet tall with crimson flowers. There is also a white and a white-pink variety; respectively the cultivated 'Alba' and 'Elegans'.
In shops: Seldom.

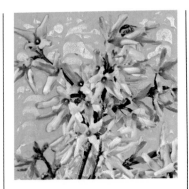

FORSYTHIA intermedia
Forsythia

Flowering period: March and April.
Colour: Golden-yellow.
Care: The well-known Forsythia is a hardy deciduous shrub which can grow to 8 feet or more with a similar spread. Forsythia is a good hedging plant and it will thrive in any ordinary garden soil. Plant this beautiful shrub in October to March in a sunny spot or part shade. For hedging, plant between October and November at 18 inch intervals. After planting remove the top third of all shoots. Pinch out when the growths are 6 inches to make the shrub bushy. Propagate with 1 feet cuttings in October.
In shops: November-May.

FREESIA
Freesia

Flowering period: January-May.
Colour: Yellow, white, purple, etcetera.
Care: This very popular cut flower is originally a South African bulbous plant grown commercially and available in bloom all year. The plant can be grown outdoors in light, rich soil and plenty of sun, although it is rather difficult, since it needs a ground temperature of 15-18°C. Usually it is grown indoors. Plant corms in April, shelter and protect. Or plant in mild areas in August or September. Freesia will flower April and May, or under glass January to April if set in boxes in your greenhouse.
In shops: All year.

GAILLARDIA aristata
Blanket flower

Flowering period: June to October.
Colour: Yellow and orange/red.
Care: The Gaillardia or Blanket flower is a familiar herbaceous border plant with colourful daisy-like flowers. It grows to 2.5 feet. It will thrive in any good, well-drained garden soil and a sunny spot. Plant the Gaillardia in the period March to May, supporting the stems where necessary. Dead-heading will prolong the flowering. Propagate by sowing seeds outdoors in the months May or June. Prick off into nursery bed and then grow on. Plant out March-April.
In shops: Autumn.

GERBERA jamesonii
Gerbera

Flowering period: May to August.
Colour: Pastel colours.
Care: Generally speaking the Gerberas are not hardy and will need greenhouse growing, except in the mildest areas. They grow to 15 inches. Grow in 8 inch pots or in a greenhouse border. In winter the temperature must not drop below 7°C, in summer minimum temperature is 16°C. Water and ventilate freely in summer giving light shade from May to September. Feed pot plants every two weeks. Propagate by division in March. Keep the Gerbera moist. Divide into single crowns.
In shops: All year round.

GLADIOLUS
Sword lily

The Sword lily or Gladiolus forms a large group of
half-hardy bulbous plants which have largely been
overtaken by a flood of hybrids, the colours of which
spread right across the spectrum. There are five main
groups, the most popular of which is the Large-
Flowered Hybrids because of their dramatic, showy
blooms. They grow up to 4 feet high and produce
almost triangular flowers which are up to 7 inches
wide. Best-known varieties include 'Oscar' (bright
red), 'Peter Pears' (peach and red) and 'Flower Song'
(yellow). The second group is the Primulinus
Hybrids which grow up to 3 feet. Characteristically
the top petal of each flower is hooded. Best-known
varieties in this group include 'Joyce' (yellow and
pink) and 'Columbine' (pink and white). Group three
is Butterfly Hybrids which grow to 4 feet and boast
close-packed flowers on the stem and striking
colours on the throat. Varieties in this third group
include 'Melodie' (pink petals, scarlet throat).
Group four is the Miniature Hybrids which grow to
2.5 feet and boast flowers that are often frilled or
ruffled. Common varieties include 'Greenbird'
(yellow). The final group is the Species that is hardier
than the others and will generally grow happily
outdoors, although they may need some frost
protection. Varieties include the beautiful 'Colvilii'
(white). Gladiolus will grow in any well-drained,
fertile soil although they will do best in a spot that
provides full sun. Planting times: March to May
(hybrids), October (species). The hybrids will flower
between July and September, while the species will
flower between April and June. Propagate by planting
cormlets in April to May. It will be two years before
the actual flowering takes place.
In shops: February-December.

GLORIOSA virescens 'Rothschildiana'
Glory lily

Flowering period: June to August.
Colour: Crimson edged with yellow.
Care: The Gloriosa is a large plant which is grown
only in a greenhouse, except in the mildest areas,
where they can survive outdoors. These tender,
tuberous-rooted perennial climbers bear a striking
bloom which has six narrow, reflexed petals curled at
the edges. The Glory lily grows to 6 feet. Plant tubers
in February or March in greenhouse border or pots.
Start at 19°C and maintain humidity. Keep the plants
moist. Feed weekly in growing season.
In shops: All year round.

GYPSOPHILA
Baby's breath

Flowering period: Summer.
Colour: White or pink.
Care: Gypsophila is the name for a group of
miniature flowers grown as rockery plants. The most
commonly-grown is Gypsophila repans. It grows to 6
inches with a spread of 2 feet. The plants flowers in
June to August by spreading a carpet of blooms and
grey/blue tinged foliage. Gypsophila is a popular cut
flower used in bouquets. It will thrive in any well-
drained soil and a sunny spot. Propagate by planting
non-flowering cuttings in a cold frame in early
summer.
In shops: All year round.

HELIANTHUS annuus
Sunflower

Flowering period: July to September.
Colour: Bright yellow.
Care: Annual sunflowers all derive from this species
but varieties differ enormously, largely in growth.
Some varieties will reach as high as 10 feet with
flowers 1 foot across. Check the seed packet you buy
carefully for sowing details. The Sunflower will thrive
in any good garden soil though it does need a sunny
spot. Sow two to three seeds at each point. Feed to
obtain maximum height.
In shops: Late summer/early autumn.

HELICHRYSUM
Everlasting

Flowering period: July-October.
Colour: Yellow, red, brown, orange, violet, pink,
white.
Care: The Helichrysum family numbers about 400
varieties, most of which come from Australia and
Africa. Grown here as an annual is the Helichrysum
bracteatum. Varieties to 3 feet tall are grown as cut
flowers; hybrids to 1-2 feet as garden plants. All
varieties are suitable as dried flowers. Sow from mid-
March in cold frame; plant out mid-May in a sunny
spot. For drying, cut off flowers with stems when they
are fully open.
In shops: Autumn.

HELICONIA
Heliconia

Flowering period: May-December.
Colour: Orange-yellow, red.
Care: About 150 varieties belong to the Heliconia
family, all native to the humid, tropical forests of
Central and South America. Grown here are the
Heliconia psittacorum (with orange-yellow flowers)
and a hybrid of the Heliconia psittacorum and the
Heliconia metallica (with red flowers). They are
grown under glass as a cut flower, in an air tempera-
ture of 25-30°C and a soil temperature of 20°C.
Water well during the growing period. Rest period is
December to March. Propagate by division.
In shops: From May to December.

HELIOPSIS
Heliopsis

Flowering period: July-October.
Colour: Orange-yellow, yellow.
Care: Heliopsis is a plant family with six varieties,
all of them native to North and Central America.
Annuals in the shops here are Heliopsis buphthal-
moides and Heliopsis helianthoides, both reaching 3
feet in height; Heliopsis scabra is a perennial, 4-6
feet tall. The plant needs a sunny spot, preferably in
light, moisture retaining soil. Give it some space as it
has a strong growth. Propagate by division.
In shops: Summer and autumn.

HELIPTERUM
Immortelle

Flowering period: June-September.
Colour: Pink, white, yellow.
Care: A herb-like plant family, native to Australia and South Africa. In this country the annual Helipterum roseum is most commonly grown. It reaches a height of 2 feet and has flowerheads measuring 2 inches across. The plant owes its attraction to its coloured leaves which shimmer like silk. Sow from late March under glass; plant out mid-May at 8 inch. To dry, cut the flowers before they fully open.
In shops: Autumn.

HIPPEASTRUM
Hippeastrum

Flowering period: January-April.
Colour: White, pink, red, orange etcetera.
Care: The Hippeastrum is a tropical and sub-tropical bulb usually available now as hybrids and only grown as greenhouse or conservatory plants because they need warmth. Plant winter and spring flowering varieties in September or October. They need a minimum temperature of 16°C. Keep the bulbs moist, but avoid too much water. Summer and autumn flowering bulbs are potted in early spring at the same temperature. Water less in September and let the bulb rest for approximately 1 month.
In shops: All year round.

HYACINTHUS orientalis
Hyacinth

Flowering period: April to May.
Colour: White, yellow, orange, pink, blue.
Care: The Hyacinthus is an indoor pot plant and outdoor bedding plant par excellence. This plant produces a wide-range of coloured blooms with a fine scent and, while bulbs are more expensive than many others, it is easy to grow. Will thrive in any good garden soil in a sunny or light shade spot which is not too dry. Plant September to October, 6 inches apart. Grows up to one foot.
In shops: Winter and spring.

HYDRANGEA macrophylla
Hydrangea

Flowering period: July to September.
Colour: Pink to blue.
Care: A species of hydrangea which forms a rounded shrub popular in gardens. Grows to 6 feet and, in mild areas, even as high as 12 feet. Garden forms include 'Blue Bird' and 'Grayswood'.
Plant in October and November or March and April. Hydrangea needs a good, loamy, moisture-retaining soil enriched with manure. A sheltered spot is best. Plant Hydrangea in the sun or part shade. Dress with peat, mulch in April.
In shops: Summer/early autumn.

IBERIS amara
Candytuft

Flowering period: May onwards.
Colour: White.
Care: Iberis or Candytuft is a hardy annual which
grows to 15 inches. It should last well into winter.
Buy 'Giant Hyacinth Flowered White' for its dense
clusters of flowers. It will thrive in ordinary well-
drained garden soil and a sunny spot. Will still do
well if soil is poor. Dead-head the plants regularly to
stimulate the flowering. Sow September to May. If
sown in autumn, protect against wintercold.
In shops: Late spring, summer, autumn.

IPHEION uniflorum
Ipheion

Flowering period: July.
Colour: Purplish blue.
Care: Ipheion grows up to 2 feet and is a reasonably
hardy plant if grown in a sunny site, especially at the
foot of a south facing wall. Plant corms in September
in groups of five or six in well-drained soil. Ipheion
can be grown in a greenhouse. Soak well after
planting and keep at minimum temperature of 7°C. In
August or September every 2/3 years you will have to
lift the plants and divide the bulbs.
In shops: April-October.

IRIS
Iris

The Iris is a vast genus of plants which can basically
be summarised in three sections. The Reticulata
group consists of dwarf plants whose stems reach up
to 6 inches high and which bloom in late winter to
early spring. Common varieties in this group include
Iris reticulata (purplish blue flowers February to
March) and Iris danfordiae (yellow flowers February
to March). The June group is distinctive because of
its thick rooted bulbs which must not be broken
when planting. They reach about 1.5 feet. Largely
neglected as a group, it boasts the splendid Iris
bucharica (cream and yellow flowers in April) and the
Iris aucheri (lilac and yellow flowers in April).
The third group is the summer-flowering Xiphium,
especially popular for cut flowers. This group grows
to 2 feet and includes the early-flowering 'Wedgewood' with its delicate pale blue flowers.
Plant Reticulata bulbs 2 inches deep in the period
September to October 4 inches apart. June bulbs are
set out in September or October 2 inches deep and
6-9 inches apart. Xiphium varieties should be
planted 4-6 inches deep in September or October
about 6 inches apart.
Iris plants like light, preferably chalk or lime soil
which is well-drained. They also like a spot with
plenty of sunlight. Surviving through the winter can
be a problem with irises. Some of them can prove
very tender. It is best to lift the bulbs after flowering.
Propagate by dividing the bulbs once the foliage has
died down. Store in a cool, but not frosty, dry place
until planting time in the autumn. Irises can be hit by
aphids when they are in store, particularly by tulip
bulb aphids. These may also infest your growing
plants, so be aware of it and check your bulbs from
time to time.
In shops: All year round.

IXIA
Corn Lily

Flowering period: June to July.
Colour: Yellow, red, blue, purple.
Care: Though Ixia is not hardy in most areas it can survive in mild regions. But generally this striking plant, which carries six-petalled star-shaped flowers in a variety of colours, is best planted in early spring and lifted after flowering, in summer. Store the bulbs in a dry place. You can also try overwintering but then you will have to cover the bulbs well. They like light, well-drained soil and a place in full sun. Plant in March 3 inches deep and 4 inches apart. Ixia grows to 1.5 feet.
In shops: Spring, summer.

KNIPHOFIA uvaria
Red Hot Poker

Flowering period: July to September.
Colour: Red, yellow, white.
Care: The Kniphofia or Red Hot Poker is a striking hardy herbaceous perennial prized for its red-tipped flowers, but which comes in a variety of other colours. Grows to 5 feet. It thrives in any well-drained garden soil but likes a spot that provides full sun. For the traditional red-tipped flower select 'Royal Standard' or 'The Rocket'. Mulch in late spring and water in dry weather. Cover with dead leaves or peat-dust in winter. Propagate by division in spring.
In shops: Summer/early autumn.

LATHYRUS odoratus
Sweet pea

Flowering period: June to September.
Colour: Pink, white or purple.
Care: This sweet-smelling annual grows up to 10 feet and should be planted at no more than 10 inches apart. It comes in a bewildering range of varieties. The Spencer varieties are the most common, choose 'Air Warden' or 'Winston Churchill'. Plant Lathyrus in any well-drained garden soil in a sunny open spot. Sow in April/May outdoors in well-manured soil or in February/March in pots in a cold frame or greenhouse.
In shops: March-August.

LAVANDULA officinalis
Old English Lavender

Flowering period: July to September.
Colour: Lavender.
Care: Distinctive-smelling hardy evergreen shrub growing to 4 feet with about the same spread. Plant Old English Lavender between September and March in ordinary, well-drained soil and in a sunny spot. If you want the Lavender to grow for hedging, plant 9-12 inches apart. If you use it for drying, pick before the flowers are fully open but when they are showing colour. Cut whole flower stalks, tie and hang them. Propagate by 4 inch cuttings in August.
In shops: Fresh or dry all year.

LIATRIS
Gayfeather

Flowering period: August to September.
Colour: Pink, pale purple.
Care: Liatris is a splendid border and cut flower plant which has densely clothed spikes bearing fluffy flowers in late summer or early autumn. It flourishes in moist, but well-drained soil. Dig in good, well rotted compost before planting in September and October or March and April. Gayfeather, which is its English name, grows to 3 feet. Remove fading flowers from the top. Liatris will disappear below ground in winter so mark their position to avoid damaging.
In shops: June-December.

LIMONIUM sinuatum
Sea Lavender

Flowering period: July-September.
Colour: Various colours.
Care: Widely grown for indoor decoration, this striking annual plant enjoys well-drained garden soil, although it will thrive in any light and medium ground. It likes a sunny spot. It grows to 2 feet and makes an ideal plant for drying. Plant out when the last frosts have gone, 1 foot apart. Propagate by sowing thinly in pots under glass in February or March. Prick off the plants and harden off before planting them in your garden.
In shops: All year round.

LILIUM
Lily

Growing lilies has traditionally been something left to a dedicated band of enthusiastic gardeners who don't mind the considerable investment of time and effort that is needed to grow them successfully. Nowadays, however, great progress has been made in producing varieties that are no longer as difficult to grow as they once were. Hybrid lilies have been bred that overcome the old problems that have daunted gardeners. Now you can grow lilies with flowers from 1 inch to 1 foot and with colours that spread right across the spectrum. They are mainly imported from the United States. They come in three main forms: bowl-shaped, trumpet-shaped and Turk's Cap-shaped. Bowl-shaped varieties of the Lilium, including Lilium auratum and Lilium speciosum, have petals that flare open to expose a wide bowl. Trumpet-shaped varieties, including Lilium longiflorum and Lilium regale are, as the name suggests, trumpet-shaped producing a basal tube. Turk's Cap-shaped varieties include Lilium amabile and Lilium hansonii, and have petals that sweep back and smallish flowers.

They can be planted any time from late summer to early spring, but October is the best month. Most lilies are stem-rooting and will need 6 inches of soil over them.

They like well-drained soil. If soil is heavy dig in peat and coarse sand. Some varieties don't like lime and some do. Consult your supplier. Do not allow the lilies to dry out in summer, water well in dry weather. Feed occasionally and mulch round the stems. Stake the lilies if they are tall varieties. Dead-head faded flowers to maintain the strength of the plant. Propagate by dividing the clumps in autumn. Replant them immediately. Divided parts may not flower the next year. Slugs may menace your plants. Beware of them.
In the shops: All year round.

LUNARIA annua
Honesty

Flowering period: April to June.
Colour: Purple.
Care: This quick-growing biennial reaches as much
as 2.5 feet, has distinctive, coarse-toothed leaves
and purple, four-petalled flowers, followed by silvery
seed pods. The Lunaria or Honesty grows best in
light soils and likes a little shade. Plant them from
September to March. Propagate by sowing seeds
outdoors in a nursery bed in the months May or
June. Thin them out and then transplant the plants.
In shops: Spring and early summer.

MATTHIOLA incana
Stock

Flowering period: June and July.
Colour: Pale purple.
Care: Stocks have been prominent in borders and
beds for hundreds of years but they still require
careful attention to grow properly. They like good
soil with a bit of chalk and full sun or partial shade.
Enrich poor soil with well-rotted manure. They will
grow up to 2 feet high. In the spring, improve flower
growth and size by adding some nitrogenous
fertiliser or a pinch of dried blood around each
established plant. Sow outdoors in April/May in a
sheltered spot. They can be susceptible to club root.
In shops: Spring.

MOLUCCELLA laevis
Bells of Ireland

Flowering period: August to September.
Colour: Insignificant white.
Care: The striking thing about this plant is the large
green bell-like calyx that surrounds the flower which
is white, small and rather insignificant. Splendid in
the garden, and as an everlasting dried flower, they
will thrive in any normal garden soil but prefer light,
rich soil and an open site. They will grow to 2 feet.
Propagate by sowing under glass in March at 15°C.
Prick off the plants into boxes and harden off under a
cold frame. Plant out the specimens in May.
Molucella can be sown outdoors in April.
In shops: Summer, autumn, winter.

MUSCARI
Grape hyacinth

Flowering period: April and May.
Colour: Deep blue, white rims.
Care: The Muscari is a useful clump-forming plant
which gives your border or rockery splendid
splashes of blue. It is also a very good cut flower. It
will thrive in full sun and any well-drained soil. It
grows to about 9 inches. Plant the Muscari in
September or October setting bulbs in groups. It can
also be grown in pots with up to 12 bulbs in one 6
inch pot. Propagate by division in autumn every
three or four years, but wait until leaves are yellow.
Replant the small bulbs immediately after division.
In shops: Late winter, spring.

NARCISSUS
Narcissus, daffodil

Officially called the narcissus this very famous plant is more likely to be called the daffodil when the central cup is as long, or longer, than the petals. It is one of the easiest plants to grow, yet one of the most delightful, bursting into colour as early as March, giving the spring garden new life. It is also a very fine cut flower. You will find daffodils or narcissi in the flower shops very early in spring-time. Generally all narcissi fall into one of twelve categories. It is a vast family, but the main types are: Trumpet narcissus, with only one large flower per stem and the trumpet as long as the petals; Large-cupped, with one flower per stem and the cup not as long as the petals; Small-cupped, with one flower per stem and a cup less than one third the length of the petals; Double, with more than one ring of petals; Triandrus, with several drooping flowers to a stem, this type is a hybrid; Cyclamineus, with one drooping flower per stem with long trumpets; Jonquilla with several flowers per stem and a cup shorter than the petals. The flowers produce a fine scent. They are often used in rock-gardens as they are sensitive to too much water; Tazetta, with several flowers per stem and a cup shorter than the often frilled petals; Poeticus which has one flower per stem and white frilled petals; Dwarf, which includes various hybrids growing up to 8 inches; Split-corona which have the corona split at least one third of its length; Miscellaneous, which includes all those not falling into other categories. Narcissi will thrive in any well-drained garden soil in a sunny spot or in light shade. Plant the bulbs in August to September, as early as possible. They will flower from March to April. In winters with long periods of frost the bulbs will have to be protected. They need manure every year.
In shops: Late winter, spring.

NERINE bowdenii
Nerine

Flowering period: September to October.
Colour: Pink.
Care: This striking variety, originally from South-Africa, is the only Nerine that can be safely grown outdoors. It has beautiful flowers and stems with hardly any leaves. However, good, well-drained garden soil and a spot that provides full sun, are essential. Plant the bulbs in April to May, 4 inches deep and 6 inches apart. Nerine will grow to 2 feet. Propagate by division of the clumps in spring, but re-plant immediately.
In shops: June-March.

NIGELLA damascena
Love-in-a-mist

Flowering period: July to September.
Colour: Blue, pink, mauve, white.
Care: Nigella, more widely known as Love-in-a-mist, is a bushy hardy annual which has become a real favourite for its delightful array of summer flowers. Grown since Elizabethan times when only blue flowers were available. Excellent for drying. Nigella needs well-drained soil and a spot in full sun or light shade. Sow in autumn or spring. The plant will also self-sow. It grows to 1.5 feet. Dead-head to increase growth.
In shops: Summer/early autumn.

ORCHIDACEAE
Orchids

An enormous family of magnificent flowers. Some varieties do require fairly rigid conditions but others are remarkably tolerant and can be grown with great success. With care and in a greenhouse the amateur gardener can derive great satisfaction and some striking blooms by growing the right varieties. Orchids can be divided into two categories, those that grow on the ground (terrestrial) and those that grow in the branches of trees or in rocks (epiphytic). The latter group, which get their nourishment from rainwater, the air and from humus in the crevices of bark, are the type that can be most easily grown by the amateur gardener. They will consist of a horizontal rhizome which produces swollen stems called pseudobulbs. Sometimes these bulbs will be single, bulb-like in appearance and producing a tuft or fan of lanceolate (lance-shaped) leaves. Others will produce a stem-like pseudobulb with joints and lanceolate or oblong leaves. One other group of epiphytes has no pseudobulbs at all, but instead has elongated stems with thick, strap-like leaves and loose-hanging aerial roots.

The terrestrial varieties have either underground tubers or fleshy roots at the base. The flowers of orchids have three petals, the third of which is like a lip and is often larger than the others. The shape and size of the lip will vary from one type to another. Sometimes it will be spurred, sometimes lobed. Its reproductive organs are confined to one organ with the pollen at the top and the ovary just below. The cultivation of orchids varies widely from type to type according to the country of origin, but generally speaking they will be grown in cool, medium or warm greenhouses. Those grown in cool greenhouses will require a minimum winter temperature of 7°C, those grown in medium greenhouses 10°C, and those in warm greenhouses 14°C. Corresponding summer temperatures are 14°C, 18°C and 22°C. They can all withstand warmer temperatures and if in doubt allow more heat rather than less. Almost all will need a good deal of humidity which is best supplied by spraying or by damping down the greenhouse. In warm conditions this will need to be done more frequently. Generally speaking epiphytic orchids like a mixture of ground bark, peat, sphagnum moss and vermiculite. Terrestrial varieties need a more loamy compost made up of equal parts by volume of coarse peat, loam, sand and moss.

Most terrestrial orchids can be grown in well-drained and crocked flower pots. Epiphytes should be grown in specially perforated pots, or directly onto pieces of tree trunk or bark. They should be attached with wire or staples. After potting do not water for about 8-10 days, then water gently for about two weeks using rainwater, until the new roots have become firmly established. In the growing season, from April to September, keep all orchids nice and moist. Terrestrials can be watered by can where they stand, topping up the compost to the rim of the pot each time. To water epiphytes submerge each pot in a bucket of water for a few minutes. When it is hot do this at least twice a week.
In shops: All year round.

ORNITHOGALUM thyrsoides
Star of Bethlehem

Flowering period: May to July.
Colour: Cream or yellow.
Care: The Star of Bethlehem is too tender to be grown outdoors and therefore this bulbous plant is usually grown as a pot plant and sold as a cut flower. It grows to a height of 18 inches and is widely cultivated in Africa to provide Europe with cut flowers. Plant the Ornithogalumbulbs in October in 8 inch pots of compost to be sure of flowers the following spring. Dead-head this specimen regularly.
In shops: May-December.

PAEONIA
Peony

Flowering period: April to July.
Colour: Variety of colours.
Care: The peony is a beautiful plant and one of the most superior of herbaceous perennials. They produce vast bowls of petals in single or double colours, depending on the variety. They can grow up to a height of 2 feet. To be sure of success choose an open, sunny spot and deeply dug, enriched soil. Plant peony in early autumn and leave the specimen alone. It is quite possible that the peony will not flower the first year, but don't transplant it. Mulch in spring, water when dry and dead-head regularly.
In shops: March-July.

PAPAVER orientale
Oriental poppy

Flowering period: May to June.
Colour: White to deep red.
Care: The Papaver or oriental poppy is a striking and dominant plant. It will overpower smaller ones in your garden. Papaver grows up to 3 feet. It likes any ordinary well-drained soil, but absolutely hates heavy land. Oriental poppy thrives in full sun. Cut down the plants to ground level at the end of the flowering season. Divide the specimens every three years. Papaver can also be propagated by root cuttings in winter.
In shops: Rare, but if so in early summer.

PHLOX paniculata
Phlox

Flowering period: July to October.
Colour: White, red, violet, orange, etcetera.
Care: The well-known Phlox is a reliable herbaceous border plant growing up to 4 feet. This specimen comes in a range of colours. It produces swathes of colour in the summer and is a prolific grower which likes any moisture retaining garden soil. Mulch the plants in the springtime and water them well when the weather is dry. Staking will be necessary for taller varieties. Cut down to 2 inches above the ground in late autumn. Propagate by division.
In shops: Late summer, autumn, winter.

PHYSALIS
Chinese Lantern

Flowering period: July to August.
Colour: Orange-red.
Care: The insignificant white flowers that this plant produces in summer turn to striking large, flame-coloured paper structures in September. The Physalis is a garden novelty and provides a splendid dried plant. It grows to 2 feet in any reasonable garden soil in a sunny spot or in part-shade. Plant the Chinese Lantern away from other plants as its underground stems are highly invasive. Cut the stems in September and hang them in a cool place if you want them for drying.
In shops: Autumn, early winter.

PHYSOSTEGIA
Obedient plant

Flowering period: July to September.
Colour: White, pink, purple.
Care: The Physostegia is certainly obedient. It is so called because of the strange way in which its striking tubular flowers will stay in most positions to which they are pushed. The obedient plant thrives in any well-drained garden soil, in a sunny spot or a place in the garden that provides partial shade. It grows to 3 feet and will usually be so prolific that it will need to be lifted and divided every three years.
In shops: Autumn, early winter.

PROTEA
Sugar bush

Flowering period: Dependent on type.
Colour: Purple, pink, yellow.
Care: The Protea is a family of plants native to Australia and Africa and containing 140 varieties. They are bushes with large clusters of unperfumed flowers enclosed in a large coloured outer leaf. They can be kept for six weeks in water and are also very attractive when dried. The flowers available in the shops here are imported from South Africa. The best known variety is the Protea cynaroides with lovely pale pink flowers measuring 1 feet across and a satin-like deep pink outer leaf.
In shops: All year round.

PRUNUS glandulosa
Prunus

Flowering period: April.
Colour: Pink or white.
Care: The Prunus is a bushy, flowering shrub, native to China, which grows to a height of 5 feet. Plant this shrub in a sheltered sunny site in early autumn when the soil is still warm. Prunus likes any ordinary well-drained soil. Being one of a wide number of ornamental almonds from the Prunus genus, its forms include the 'Albo-plena' which has double-white flowers and the 'Sinensis' which has double bright pink flowers.
In shops: Winter and spring.

ROSA
Rose

Flowering period: Depends on the variety, the early roses flower at the end of spring; there are varieties that flower until the frost period starts.
Colour: Many, red, white, yellow and all colours in between.
Care: The story of the rose spans millions of years – its beauty and fragrance have inspired poets and soldiers, painters and politicians through the centuries. The number of species surviving may well be as high as 250. They are found wild only in the Northern Hemisphere and really only grow well in temperate climes. The cultivation of roses has always been very important in China and Persia. The roses served as a base for the rose-oil people love so much in these countries. Most roses you can buy in flower shops nowadays are varieties of the hybrid tea roses. They come in beautiful red, pink or yellow colours. From the bewildering array of species available roses can be divided into various categories according to their characteristics.
Species roses. This category includes the ancestors of the modern rose, wild roses from various parts of the world. They are usually strongly resistant to pests and diseases and have a single flower with five petals. They are usually hardy and deciduous.
Old roses. They are early hybrids of the rose species and these specimens were commonly-grown before the arrival of the Hybrid tea rose. They have a short flowering season but produce strikingly fragrant flowers. These old roses are divided into 13 sub-groups according to parentage.
Hybrid Tea roses. These are the successors to the Old roses. They have freely-produced flowers, show a long flowering season (June to October) and make excellent cut flowers. They thrive in sunny spots or partial shade. They are hardy, deciduous and with strong prickly stems. Unfortunately the hybrid Tea Roses are prone to pests and diseases.
Floribunda roses. To this group belong the hardy, deciduous shrubs with foliage similar to Hybrid Tea-roses but their stems are more branched.
Modern shrub-roses. This variety is a hybrid of Species and Old roses. They have an informal growth and are usually suitable for hedging or arches. These roses require only light pruning.
Climbers and ramblers. This special variety includes a wide range of climbing roses and ramblers. They have hooked thorns in their stems.

Miniature roses. These are small shrublets which have almost thornless stems. True miniature roses are derived from the dwarf China semi-double rose, from which the miniatures have inherited a long flowering season and a fine beauty. They are hardy, and can also be grown in pots.

It can be seen from this brief description of the many varieties of roses that widely differing methods of cultivation will be needed. However some basic advice can be given that is common to all roses. They will all need good drainage and open, sunny positions. They do not like windy spots, as this can loosen the roots, and they need plenty of water. If the soil is poor then dig in plenty of well-rotted compost to retain moisture, and aid the drainage. Only use animal manure in the bottom spit because it is harmful to the roots of the roses. Top dress the rose-bed with peat that is mixed with hop manure. Prepare the bed a good month before you plant the roses, which should be done in October and November. Take care to space the roses according to their nature and habit. Roses that are not too vigorous can obviously be planted closer together than others. To plant, make up a mixture of 2 gallons moist peat to one handful of bone-meal. Dig the appropriate sized hole. Place this planting mixture to a depth of 2 inches in the hole and mix it with the soil. Place the rose of your choice in position with the union of stock and scion just below soil level. Spread out the roots and continue adding planting mixture until the roots are covered. Add the remainder of the soil and tread it firmly down. Standard roses will need to be firmly staked and tied. Dead-head the plants as soon as the roses have faded. Mulch, preferably with rotted cow or horse manure. When pruning finish all cuts cleanly and cut directly above a bud and close to it.

Roses are susceptible to attack by greenfly, mildew and blackspot. Ask your garden centre for information about the best methods of protection. The so-called 'rose fatigue' is caused by a worm that can develop quickly when roses are planted. The first generation of roses will not suffer from this, but if you plant new roses on the same spot these will be badly attacked by the worms. When you want to renew your rose bed or border you can prevent this by planting the ground with African marigolds during the final year. These give off a powder that kills the worms. After flowering, dig them well in and lift the rose bushes.
In shops: All year round.

RUDBECKIA
Coneflower

Flowering period: August to October.
Colour: Golden orange.
Care: The Rudbeckia is called coneflower because of the dark, cone-shaped centre of the flower. This is a splendid, late-flowering plant which produces masses of large blooms. The coneflower is ideal for obtaining cut flowers. The plant likes any well-drained soil and will flower in a sunny spot or in light shade. It grows up to 3 feet and can be propagated by sowing outside in mid-April.
In shops: Autumn and early winter.

SAPONARIA
Soapwort

Flowering period: July to September.
Colour: White and pink.
Care: The Saponaria or soapwort is an intrusive but charming plant for an informal cottage garden. It thrives in any reasonable garden soil, provided it is not too moist, in sun or light shade. Saponaria will grow undisturbed for years, but it will spring up all over your garden. This plant can be simply propagated by dividing (the poisonous!) clumps in autumn or spring. Cut down the stems to ground level in autumn.
In shops: Summer (rarely sold).

SCABIOSA
Scabious

Flowering period: June to October.
Colour: Lavender.
Care: The Scabiosa gives you large blooms of large-headed lavender flowers which are not abundant but which bloom for a long period. The flowers are ideal for indoor arrangements. This plant likes well-drained soil and a spot in your garden with sun or partial shade. Plant the Scabiosa in spring, dead-head regularly and cut down the stems when the flowering season ends. Scabiosa grows to 3 feet. Propagate by division of the clumps in the spring.
In shops: Summer, early autumn.

SOLIDAGO
Golden rod

Flowering period: July to September.
Colour: Golden.
Care: The Solidago or Golden rod is a delightful, bright-flowering perennial which grows in swathes of colour through summer and into autumn. The flowers look like panicles and can be dried. This plant likes any well-drained soil, sun or light shade. It can grow to 7 feet, so it may need some unobtrusive staking. Mulch the plants in spring preferably under the clump, so it may need to be lifted, water when dry and cut down the shoots in autumn. Divide the plants in autumn.
In shops: Late summer, autumn.

STRELITZIA
Bird of paradise flower

Flowering period: April and May.
Colour: Orange and blue.
Care: The bird of paradise flower as its beautiful name implies, is one of the most striking flowers you will come across. This tender evergreen perennial needs greenhouse growing. It grows up to 4 feet. Grow Strelitzia in pots in a greenhouse border at 10°C in winter keeping the plant nearly dry but be careful its leaves do not wither. Water freely in spring and summer, reducing again from September on. Ventilate your greenhouse when temperature exceeds 18°C. Liquid feed in May to September.
In shops: All year round.

SYRINGA vulgaris
Lilac

Flowering period: May and June.
Colour: Lilac.
Care: The Syringa vulgaris is a hardy deciduous shrub which grows to 12 feet, with a spread up to 10 feet. Plant this shrub between October and November in a sunny spot or partial shade. They will thrive in fertile garden soil and will need little attention once they are well established. The Syringa is ideal for hedging, set at intervals of 6-10 feet. Prune by removing faded flowers from October. Cut down the overgrown bushes to 3 feet in wintertime.
In shops: Winter, early spring.

TULIPA
Tulips

Flowering period: Spring.
Colour: A vast variety.
Care: Tulips are magnificent spring-flowering plants that give great splashes of rich colours at a time when less hardy summer bedding plants are still struggling to come alive. Originating from Turkey the tulip has more recently become closely associated with Holland, where specialist growers cultivate hundreds of different varieties. All tulips have certain characteristics. They grow from rounded bulbs with thin outer skins and a pointed nose. Most tulips, though not all, carry single blooms which are goblet-shaped.
Garden hybrids fall into nine categories: single early, which grow to 16 inches and flower in mid-April, but have small blooms: double early which grow to 16 inches, flower in mid-April and are long lasting; Triumph which grow to 24 inches, flower April to May and were obtained by crossing single earlies with the Darwin-tulips. They are strong-stemmed; Darwin, originally from Belgium, which grow to 30 inches, flower early to mid-May and are strong-stemmed with large flowers (most common garden tulip); Lily-flowered tulips which grow to 2 feet. They flower from April to May, have long flowers and strong stems; Cottage, this tulip reaches a height of 30 inches and flowers in early May showing old fashioned, long, egg-shaped blooms.
Rembrandt is a tulip that will be 24 inches high, flower in mid-May and have petals that are streaked with a second colour, actually caused by a kind of virus; Parrot, 28 inches high, flowers in mid-May and has large frilled flowers on rather weak stems; Double-late, 24 inches, flowers appear in late-May, they are very large and need protection from the wind. Species varieties are less commonly grown. Tulips like well-drained soil and full sun. Plant the bulbs in November to December by digging them 6 inches deep and up to 8 inches apart.
Propagate them by removing bulblets at lifting time (after flowering in summer), store the bulbs and replant them in a different spot in your garden (because of diseases) in autumn.
In shops: Winter and spring.

VERBASCUM
Mullein

Flowering period: June to August.
Colour: Yellow, pink, white, apricot.
Care: Verbascum are a commonly grown border species. They do not like rich soil. The Hybrids tend to be short-lived. You can plant Verbascum in ordinary, well-drained soil, choosing a spot in full sun in October or in March or April. It will grow up to 5 feet, so stake the tall varieties. Cut down the stems to ground level in November. The Verbascum-plants will need to be replaced from time to time. Propagate them by taking root cuttings in winter.
In shops: Rare, but in summer.

VIBURNUM opulus
Viburnum

Flowering period: May and June.
Colour: White.
Care: The Viburnum is a deciduous, upright, bushy plant growing to 15 feet with a spread of similar proportions. Its flowers are followed by translucent red berries. Virburnum needs good, moist garden soil. If you grow this plant for the berries it will do better in twos or threes. Shelter the bush from the wind and frosts, but be sure to place it in full sun. Plant Viburnum in October to March. Propagate by 4 inch heel cuttings.
In shops: Spring, early summer.

ZANTEDESCHIA aethiopica
Arum Lily

Flowering period: May and June.
Colour: White.
Care: The Arum Lily is a tender greenhouse plant. Some forms can be grown outside in mild areas. It is notable for a striking white sheathing bract which has a yellow fleshy spike. The Zantedeschia grows to 3 feet. Grow the plants in 10 inch pots, cover rhizomes with 3 inches of soil and water after planting in spring. The plants can be moved outside in June. In autumn the Zantedeschia needs a period of rest, do not water it then. In January it starts to grow again. During this period feed regularly.
In shops: Spring, summer.

ZINNIA elegans
Youth and old age

Flowering period: July to October.
Colour: Various colours.
Care: The Zinnia is a delightful annual which comes in a variety of colours but which needs fertile soil and a good, warm summer for best results. In compost-enriched garden soil and a spot in full sun this fine plant can reach a height of 2.5 feet. Plant out only when the danger of frost is gone. Cut blooms, which have strong stems, last well in water. The Daisy-like flowers of this plant can be single, double or semi-double.
In shops: Autumn, early winter.

FLOWERING PERIODS

Flowering periods
In the following schedule you can find almost all the flowers mentioned in the foto-section of this book. Unless otherwise indicated, by flowering period we mean the natural flowering period. Advanced professional cultivation methods make it nowadays often possible to trade the flowers also in other periods of the year.

	Jan	Feb	Mar	Apr	May	Jun	Jul	Aug	Sep	Oct	Nov	Dec
Acacia dealbata	O	O	O									O
Achillea filipendulina							O	O				
Aconitum napellus							O	O				
Agapanthus campanulatus								O	O			
Alchemilla mollis						O	O	O				
Allium giganteum						O						
Alstroemeria aurantiaca						O	O	O	O			
Amaranthus caudatus							O	O	O	O		
Amaryllis belladonna									O	O		
Anaphalis margaritacea								O				
Anemone coronaria			O	O								
Anthemis tinctoria						O	O	O	O			
Anthurium andreanum					O	O	O	O	O			
Antirrhinum majus							O	O	O	O	O	
Artemisia ludoviciana							O	O	O			
Arum italicum									O	O	O	
Asclepias tuberosa							O	O				
Aster novae-angliae									O	O		
Aster novi-belgii									O	O		
Astilbe						O	O	O				
Astrantia major						O	O					
Bouvardia x domestica						O	O	O	O	O	O	
Calendula officinalis					O	O	O	O	O	O	O	
Callicarpa bodinieri							O					
Callistephus chinensis							O	O	O	O	O	
Campanula medium						O	O	O	O			
Celosia argentea							O	O	O			
Centaurea cyanus						O	O	O	O			
Centaurea macrocephala						O	O					
Centaurea moschata var. imperialis						O	O	O	O			
Cheiranthus cheiri				O	O	O						
Chelone obliqua								O	O			
Chrysanthemum carinatum						O	O	O	O			
Chrysanthemum coccineum (Pyrethrum roseum)					O	O	O					
Chrysanthemum indicum/morifolium hybr.									O	O	O	
Chrysanthemum maximum						O	O	O				
Chrysanthemum segetum							O	O	O			
Clarkia elegans							O	O	O			
Convallaria majalis				O	O							
Coreopsis tinctoria							O	O	O			
Cosmos bipinnatus								O	O			
Crocosmia x crocosmiiflora							O	O	O			

FLOWERING PERIODS

	Jan	Feb	Mar	Apr	May	Jun	Jul	Aug	Sep	Oct	Nov	Dec
Cyclamen persicum	O	O								O	O	O
Cynara scolymus							O	O				
Dahlia variabilis							O	O	O			
Delphinium						O	O	O				
Dianthus barbatus						O	O					
Dianthus caryophyllus hybr. Chabaud							O	O		O	O	
Dipsacus							O					
Doronicum				O	O	O						
Echinops							O	O				
Eremurus robustus					O	O						
Erigeron							O	O				
Eryngium alpinum							O	O				
Eschscholzia californica							O	O	O	O	O	
Euphorbia fulgens	O	O	O							O	O	O
Filipendula purpurea						O	O					
Forsythia			O	O								
Freesia (indoor)	O	O	O	O								
Freesia (outdoor)				O	O							
Gaillardia							O	O	O	O		
Gerbera jamesonii					O	O	O	O				
Gladiolus							O	O	O			
Gloriosa virescens 'Rothschildiana'						O	O	O				
Gypsophila						O	O	O				
Helianthus annuus							O	O	O			
Helichrysum							O	O	O	O		
Heliconia					O	O	O	O	O	O	O	O
Heliopsis							O	O	O	O		
Helipterum						O	O	O	O			
Hippeastrum	O	O	O	O								
Hyacinthus orientalis				O	O							
Hydrangea macrophylla							O	O	O			
Iberis amara				O	O							
Ipheion uniflorum							O					
Iris*		O	O	O	O	O	O	O				
Ixia						O	O					
Kniphofia uvaria							O	O				
Lathyrus odoratus							O	O	O	O		
Lavendula officinalis							O	O	O			
Liatris							O	O				
Lilium						O	O	O				
Limonium sinuatum							O	O	O			
Lunaria annua				O	O	O						
Matthiola incana							O	O				
Molucella laevis								O	O			
Muscari				O	O							
Narcissus			O	O	O							
Nerine bowdenii									O	O		
Nigella damascena							O	O	O			

FLOWERING PERIODS/AVAILABILITY IN SHOPS

	Jan	Feb	Mar	Apr	May	Jun	Jul	Aug	Sep	Oct	Nov	Dec
Ornithogalum thyrsoides					○	○	○					
Paeonia				○	○	○						
Papaver orientale					○	○						
Phlox paniculata							○	○	○	○		
Physalis							○	○				
Physostegia							○	○	○			
Prunus glandulosa				○								
Rosa★					○	○	○	○	○	○	○	
Rudbeckia								○	○	○		
Saponaria★					○	○	○	○	○	○		
Scabiosa						○	○	○	○	○		
Solidago							○	○	○			
Strelitzia				○	○							
Syringa vulgaris					○	○						
Tulipa			○	○	○							
Verbascum						○	○	○				
Viburnum opulus					○	○						
Zantedeschia aethiopica					○	○						
Zinnia elegans							○	○	○	○		

★ Dependent on species and variety

Availability in shops

	Spring	Summer	Autumn	Winter
Acacia dealbata	○			○
Achillea filipendulina		○	○	
Aconitum napellus		○	◀	
Agapanthus campanulatus		▶	◀	
Alchemilla mollis			○	
Allium giganteum	○	○	○	
Alstroemeria aurantiaca	○	○	○	○
Amaranthus caudatus		▶	○	
Amaryllis belladonna	○	▶	◀	
Anaphalis margaritacea		○		
Anemone coronaria	○	○		▶
Anthemis			○	
Anthurium andreanum	○	○	○	○
Antirrhinum majus		○	◀	
Arum italicum			○	◀
Asclepias tuberosa		▶	◀	
Aster		▶	○	
Astilbe		▶	○	
Astrantia major			○	
Banksia	○	○	○	○
Bouvardia x domestica	▶	○	○	◀
Calendula officinalis		○		
Callicarpa bodinieri	○		○	
Callistephus chinensis		○	◀	
Campanula medium	▶	◀		
Celosia argentea	○	○	○	

AVAILABILITY IN SHOPS

	Spring	Summer	Autumn	Winter
Centaurea		○		
Cheiranthus cheiri	◗	◖		
Chelone obliqua			○	
Chrysanthemum coccineum	◗	◖		
Chrysanthemum indicum/morifolium hybr.	○	○	○	○
Chrysanthemum segetum		○		
Clarkia elegans		○	○	
Convallaria majalis	○	○	○	○
Coreopsis tinctoria		○	○	
Cosmos bipinnatus		○	◗	
Crocosmia x crocosmiiflora		○	◖	
Cyclamen persicum			○	○
Cynara scolymus		○	○	
Dahlia variabilis		○	◖	
Delphinium		○		
Dianthus barbatus	◗	◖		
Dianthus caryophyllus hybr. Chabaud	○	○	○	○
Dipsacus		○	◖	
Doronicum		○		
Echinops			○	
Eremurus robustus		○		
Erigeron			○	
Eryngium alpinum			○	
Eschscholzia californica		○	◖	
Euphorbia fulgens	○	○	○	○
Forsythia	◖		◗	○
Freesia	○	○	○	○
Gaillardia		○		
Gerbera jamesonii	○	○	○	○
Gladiolus	○	○	○	
Gloriosa virescens 'Rothschildiana'	○	○	○	○
Gypsophila	○	○	○	○
Helianthus annuus		◗	◖	
Helichrysum			○	
Heliconia	◗	○	○	
Heliopsis		○	○	
Helipterum			○	
Hippeastrum	○	○	○	○
Hyacinthus orientalis	◖		◗	○
Hydrangea macrophylla	○	○	○	
Iberis amara	○	○	○	
Ipheion uniflorum	○	○	◖	
Iris	○	○	○	○
Ixia	○	○		
Kniphofia uvaria		○	◖	
Lathyrus odoratus	◗	○		
Lavendula officinalis	○	○	○	○

AVAILABILITY IN SHOPS/AVAILABLE COLOURS

	Spring	Summer	Autumn	Winter
Liatris		○	○	
Lilium	○	○	○	○
Limonium sinuatum	○	○	○	○
Lunaria annua	○	◖		
Matthiola incana	○			
Molucella laevis		○	○	○
Muscari	○			○
Narcissus	○			○
Nerine bowdenii		○	○	○
Nigella damascena		○	◖	
Orchidaceae	○	○	○	○
Ornithogalum thyrsoides		○	○	○
Paeonia	○	◖		
Phlox paniculata		○		
Physalis			○	◖
Physostegia			○	◖
Protea	○	○	○	○
Prunus glandulosa	○			○
Rosa	○	○	○	○
Rudbeckia			○	◖
Scabiosa		○	◖	
Solidago	○	○	○	○
Strelitzia	○	○	○	○
Syringa vulgaris	◖			○
Tulipa	○			○
Viburnum opulus	◖			○
Zantedeschia aethiopica	○	○		
Zinnia elegans			○	◖

○ The whole period　◖ First half of the period　◗ Second half of the period

Available colours

	White	Yellow	Blue	Violet	Orange	Pink	Red
Acacia dealbata		○					
Achillea filipendulina		○					
Aconitum napellus				○			
Agapanthus campanulatus	○		○				
Alchemilla mollis		○					
Allium giganteum				○			
Alstroemeria aurantiaca		○			○	○	○
Amaranthus caudatus				○			
Amaryllis belladonna	○	○				○	
Anaphalis margaritacea	○						
Anemone coronaria	○		○				○
Anthemis tinctoria		○					
Anthurium andreanum	○					○	○
Antirrhinum majus	○	○			○	○	○
Artemisia ludoviciana		○					
Arum italicum	○						○
Asclepias tuberosa					○		

	White	Yellow	Blue	Violet	Orange	Pink	Red
Aster novae-angliae			O			O	O
Aster novi-belgii	O		O	O		O	O
Astilbe	O					O	O
Astrantia major	O					O	O
Banksia		O					
Bouvardia x domestica	O					O	O
Callendula officinalis		O			O		
Callicarpa bodinieri						O	
Callistephus chinensis	O		O	O		O	O
Cheiranthus cheiri	O	O		O	O		O
Chelone obliqua						O	
Chrysanthemum coccineum	O	O				O	O
Chrysanthemum indicum/morifolium hybr.	O	O		O	O	O	O
Chrysanthemum maximum	O						
Chrysanthemum segetum		O					
Clarkia elegans	O		O	O	O	O	O
Convallaria majalis	O						
Coreopsis tinctoria		O					
Cosmos bipinnatus	O					O	O
Crocosmia x crocosmiiflora		O				O	O
Cyclamen	O						O
Cynara scolymus				O			
Dahlia variabilis	O	O		O	O	O	O
Delphinium	O		O	O		O	
Dianthus barbatus	O			O		O	O
Dianthus caryophyllus hybr. Chabaud	O	O		O	O	O	O
Dipsacus				O			
Doronicum		O					
Echinops			O				
Eremurus robustus		O					
Erigeron			O	O			
Eryngium alpinum			O				
Eschscholzia californica		O			O		
Euphorbia fulgens	O				O	O	O
Filipendula purpurea	O					O	O
Forsythia		O					
Freesia	O	O	O	O			O
Gaillardia		O			O		
Gerbera jamesonii	O	O		O	O	O	O
Gladiolus	O	O		O	O		O
Gloriosa virescens 'Rothschildiana'							O
Gypsophila	O					O	
Helianthus annuus		O					
Helichrysum	O	O		O	O	O	O
Heliconia					O		O
Heliopsis		O			O		
Helipterum	O	O				O	
Hippeastrum	O					O	O
Hyacinthus orientalis	O			O		O	O

AVAILABLE COLOURS

	White	Yellow	Blue	Violet	Orange	Pink	Red
Hydrangea macrophylla			○			○	
Iberis amara	○						
Ipheion uniflorum	○			○			
Iris	○	○	○	○		○	
Ixia		○	○	○			○
Kniphofia uvaria	○	○					○
Lathyrus odoratus	○			○		○	○
Lavendula officinalis				○			
Liatris				○		○	
Lilium	○	○			○	○	
Limonium sinuatum	○	○	○		○	○	○
Lunaria annua				○			
Matthiola incana	○	○		○		○	○
Molucella laevis	○						
Muscari				○			
Narcissus	○	○					
Nerine bowdenii						○	
Nigella damascena	○		○	○			
Ornithogalum thyrsoides	○					○	○
Paeonia	○	○					
Papaver orientale	○				○	○	○
Phlox paniculata	○		○	○	○	○	○
Physalis	○						
Protea		○		○		○	○
Prunus glandulosa	○					○	
Rosa	○	○	○		○	○	○
Rudbeckia		○				○	
Saponaria	○						
Scabiosa			○	○		○	○
Solidago		○					
Strelitzia				○	○		
Syringa vulgaris	○			○			
Tulipa	○	○				○	○
Verbascum	○	○				○	○
Viburnum opulus	○						
Zantedeschia aethiopica	○						
Zinnia elegans	○	○			○	○	○

INDEX OF PLANT NAMES

INDEX OF PLANT NAMES